W9-CAG-980

Sizzle!

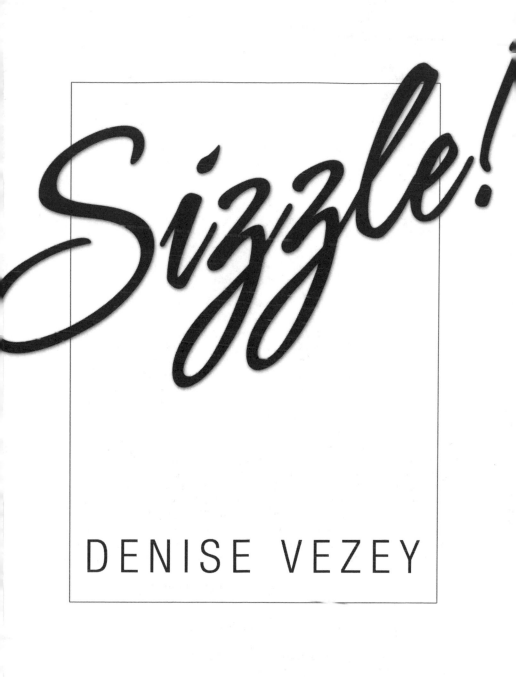

Sizzle!

DENISE VEZEY

LIFE JOURNEY®

Bringing Home the Message for Life

COOK COMMUNICATIONS MINISTRIES
Colorado Springs, Colorado • Paris, Ontario
KINGSWAY COMMUNICATIONS LTD
Eastbourne, England

Life Journey® is an imprint of
Cook Communications Ministries, Colorado Springs, CO 80918
Cook Communications, Paris, Ontario
Kingsway Communications, Eastbourne, England

SIZZLE!
© 2006 by Denise Vezey

All rights reserved. No part of this book may be reproduced without written permission, except for brief quotations in books and critical reviews. For information,
write Cook Communications Ministries, 4050 Lee Vance View, Colorado Springs,
CO 80918.

Cover Design: TrueBlue Design/Sandy Flewelling
Cover Photo: ©istockphoto

First Printing, 2006
Printed in the United States of America

2 3 4 5 6 7 8 9 10 Printing/Year 10 09 08 07 06

Unless otherwise noted, Scripture quotations are taken from the HOLY BIBLE,
NEW INTERNATIONAL VERSION®. Copyright © 1973, 1978, 1984 International
Bible Society. Used by permission of Zondervan. All rights reserved. Verses
marked TLB are taken from *The Living Bible*, © 1971, Tyndale House Publishers,
Wheaton, IL 60189. Used by permission. Scripture quotations marked (NLT) are
taken from the Holy Bible, New Living Translation, copyright © 1996. Used by
permission of Tyndale House Publishers, Inc., Wheaton, Illinois 60189. All rights
reserved. Scripture quotations marked (NASB) taken from the New American
Standard Bible®, Copyright © 1960, 1962, 1963, 1968, 1971, 1972, 1973, 1975, 1977,
1995 by The Lockman Foundation. Used by permission. (www.Lockman.org.);
Scripture quotations marked AB taken from the Amplified® Bible, Copyright ©
1954, 1958, 1962, 1964, 1965, 1987 by The Lockman Foundation. Used by permission. (www.Lockman.org.), Scripture quotations marked MSG are taken from *The
Message*. Copyright © 1993, 1994, 1995, 1996, 2000, 2001, 2002. Used by permission
of NavPress Publishing Group. Scripture quotations marked (PH) are taken from J.
B. Phillips: *The New Testament in Modern English*, revised editions © J.B. Phillips,
1958, 1960, 1972, permission of Macmillan Publishing Co. and Collins Publishers.

Library of Congress Cataloging-in-Publication Data

Vezey, Denise.
    Sizzle! : seven secrets to reignite your marriage / Denise Vezey.
      p. cm.
    Includes bibliographical references.
    ISBN 0-7814-4202-8
    1. Wives--Religious life. 2. Marriage--Religious aspects--Christianity. 3. Sex in
marriage--Religious aspects--Christianity. I. Title.
BV4528.15.V49 2006
248.8'435--dc22
                                    2005022013

To Stu:

*Your passionate nature has kept our marriage
sizzling all these years!
Thanks for the support (laundry) and especially
for your deep love for me.*

Contents

Acknowledgments

To Cook Communications Ministries, for your continued belief in my projects and me. You published my children's series, Getting to Know God, and then allowed me to try my hand at this, my first nonfiction book for women. I am deeply indebted to your ministry and hope our partnership continues to be as beneficial for you as it has been for me.

Next, my heartfelt thanks and gratitude go to my editor, Mary McNeil, and to corporate publicity director, Michele Tennesen. You both grasped the core concept of this book—*your marriage doesn't have to be perfect to be wonderful*—and felt this was a message worth getting out. Mary, your professional expertise, phone calls, prayers, and emotional support have meant the world to me. You're more than just an editor; you are also my friend.

To Linda Dillow and Lorraine Pintus, for paving the way. Your work, your ministry, and especially your friendship have greatly enriched my life. Your book *Intimate Issues* was the textbook for much of my research. May God bless both of you and your families in all you do.

To my own family, Stu, Luke, Joy, Brynne, and Andrew, for letting me off the hook while I wrote this book. You gave me the freedom to take off my "mom" hat and write. I love all of you so much, and I promise I'll start cooking again now that it's finished!

To my Lord and Savior, Jesus Christ, praise and thanksgiving for meeting me in every way and supplying every need so this work could be completed. I pray that You will be glorified by marriages that are strengthened and helped through this book.

To all the women who shared your "secrets," for opening your hearts to me. It is a privilege I do not take lightly, and I know *Sizzle!* could not have been written without you. Thank you, too, for allowing me to share your stories with others so they, too, will be blessed.

Foreword

When I see the word *sizzle*, a picture flashes before my eyes of street vendors in China, who can sense just the right moment to throw meat and veggies into their perfectly prepared woks. The book you are holding is called *Sizzle!*, and although it's not about Chinese cooking, it does offer the ingredients necessary to reignite your marriage.

Lest you think that sizzle in a marriage only refers to burning a sexual flame between husband and wife, think again. Denise Vezey sets forth the emotional sparks that prepare the way for sexual intimacy. With honesty and vulnerability, she unwraps seven time-tested secrets that will ignite emotional and sexual sizzling in your marriage:

Letting Go of Perfection teaches you how to realistically move forward even if you and your husband are *very* different. I wish I'd learned this secret when I was a young bride—it would have saved me heartache and saved my husband from a wife who tried to "remake" him to be like her!

Language of Lovers applies the five love languages in a concise and motivational way. I know I'm ready to seek new ways to love my husband the way he desires to be loved.

Laugh and Play set me on the path to rediscover recreation in our marriage. No matter how many children are wrapped around your knees, recreation and relaxation are necessary in your relationship.

Life's Little Luxuries is chock-full of practical tips from how to find privacy to becoming your husband's "vacation wife." With four kids, a dog, and a husband who works out of the home, Denise understands what it's like.

Many women enter marriage with baggage from the past and often the weight of guilt keeps them from sexual freedom with their mate. *Liberated for Love* takes you on a healing journey to freedom. This isn't a philosophical journey but a practical one in which prayers and projects help you throw off the chains of bondage and be free.

Lighten Up! gives you freedom to rejoice in abandoned lovemaking while *Loyalty for a Lifetime* ties everything together. After reading this secret, you will think more deeply about your wedding vows and how they apply to you now.

I highly recommend this book to you. Making the choice to read *Sizzle!* and do the projects with your husband will set you on an intentional adventure to discover deeper intimacy in your marriage.

Linda Dillow

Author of Creative Counterpart *and co-author of* Intimate Issues

Introduction

Last February I left our house in Monument, Colorado (elevation 7,240 feet), in the semi-darkness of a freezing snowstorm to drive to Lookout Mountain Church to present my "Secrets to Make Your Marriage Sizzle" message. Try as I might to convince MOPS coordinators and women's ministry leaders that I can speak on a wide range of topics, my "Sizzle" talk is the most frequently requested.

On this particular morning, the hour-and-a-half drive turned into a three-hour ordeal as icy roads and blinding snow turned the highway into a parking lot. I gripped the steering wheel, nerves taut, and asked the Lord, "God, in the whole scope of life, in light of eternity and famine in Africa, are sizzling marriages truly important to *You?*" I often struggle with the feeling that my "Sizzle" talk is insignificant when compared to the many difficult issues women face today.

When I arrived at the church more than an hour late, to my astonishment the parking lot was full! Even on a morning with snow blowing and temperatures hovering around sixteen degrees, women had bundled up their preschoolers and braved the elements to get fresh inspiration for their marriages.

In the months that followed my heartfelt cry for affirmation that "Secrets to Make Your Marriage Sizzle" did indeed have significance in God's sight, He graciously complied. Beginning that day—and with every speaking engagement that followed—the

Lord sent woman after woman to me to share struggles in her marriage. These women said they needed the hope and tools for intimacy this talk offered.

Kaitlin's husband had made love to her only twice in the last three years. Trisha said she and her husband remained good friends and their marriage was stable, but much of the passion and romance had disappeared. Beth cringed in embarrassment as she confided her yearlong attraction to another man. Carrie, who had been married before, desperately desired for her second marriage to work but confessed she often felt confused and ambivalent toward her new husband. Andrea experienced the horrors of sexual abuse as a child and now didn't care if she ever made love with her husband, even though he was a tender, sweet, and godly man. And broken Sandra struggled to hold her marriage together by herself and didn't realize the Savior of the world stood by, ready and able to help her, if only she would reach out to Him.

Do you realize what a powerful, silent witness a strong, loving, and faithful marriage can be? Even the grocery clerk at your local store would probably be amazed to learn you and your spouse beat the odds in this day and age and remain not only married but also deeply in love.

Join me on this great adventure, will you? Seek to be intentional and fan the flames of intimacy and passion in your marriage. Dare to put your relationship with your husband first, right after your commitment to God. Get ready to be amazed at the warmth and romance that will result. Learn exciting, new ways to turn up the temperature around your home, and be reminded of some reliable truths you may have heard before. In the midst of it all, know that I am praying for you and your husband as you strive to honor God and become a bright light in a dark world through your unveiled love for one another.

LET GO OF PERFECTION

If you wait for perfect conditions, you will never get anything done.

Ecclesiastes 11:4 TLB

My marriage feels perfect today. Early this morning, my husband loaded up our jet skis, and we headed to a nearby lake with our last two at-home teenagers and my daughter's boyfriend, Tim. The sky is an amazing watercolor blue (my dad says they don't even make that color of sky in California!). A few wispy white clouds, which will probably develop into thunderstorms later this afternoon, hang high above us. The water is cool, but after all, this is Memorial Day in Colorado at four thousand feet, so we're not complaining.

Even the little tiff my husband, Stu, and I got into over a dirt road to the cove I *know* doesn't exist but he insisted was there (it wasn't) doesn't mar the profound sense of peace and contentment I feel today. On days like this, our marriage *feels* perfect. Have we truly experienced the problems and issues we've faced over the years, or did I just imagine them? Did that nasty argument we had right before my last trip to California really happen, or was it just a bad dream from too much lasagna at dinner? All the spats, disagreements, hurtful words, and painful silences seem like a blur today, a misty mirage floating in the background of my mind.

Webster's defines perfection as "freedom from fault or defect," "an exemplification of supreme excellence," and "the quality or state of being saintly."[1] Neither Stu nor I nor our marriage, for that matter, meets those definitions. But whenever I give my "Sizzle" talk and ask, "Does anyone in this room have a perfect marriage?" at least one woman raises her hand. At that point, I invite *her* to take over the meeting, because she will probably be a lot more help to the audience than I could be! You see, God had so much to teach me precisely because my marriage *isn't* perfect.

From Sizzle to Fizzle

Stu and I have been married for more than twenty-four years. We met in college just a month or so after I became a Christian. We dated for three months, broke up for six months, then got engaged and married six months later. As you can tell, we didn't have a very long or a very stable courtship. We worked together in a high school ministry during the months we didn't date, so in our opinion we knew one another well enough to marry. The pastor who did our premarital counseling apparently agreed.

Just one year after our wedding, I became pregnant with our first child, Luke. Three more children followed in quick succession, with the end result of four children in five years and three of those children in less than three years! Every one of those precious bundles was wanted and loved, but I felt like a walking zombie during those years.

My husband tried to be helpful around the house, but he often worked twelve to sixteen hours a day just to provide the bare necessities for our growing family. We lived in the Bay Area of California at the time, which was and still is one of the most expensive areas in the country in which to live. Many nights he would come home for dinner only to return to his office.

Sadly, in the five years I had our babies, both of our mothers and grandmothers died. I don't have any sisters, so the responsibility of caring for our youngsters fell completely on my shoulders. It was a devastating time, emotionally and physically.

In the midst of this difficult time, we decided to get away for two nights at a bed and breakfast in beautiful northern California. I daydreamed about the crisp mountain air; towering, forest green pines; the wonderful absence of cooking meals or washing dishes; and the silence of not being awakened in the middle of the night by a small child. I *knew* it was going to be perfect.

On the way to our dream getaway, however, we had a full-blown argument—a "nuclear explosion" as we used to call them. If we hadn't been traveling down the highway at seventy miles per hour, I'm sure I would have jumped out!

You see, my husband and I are both very expressive people. When we're in love, we are quite passionate and romantic. And when we're angry, well, it isn't a pretty sight. In fact, much to our chagrin, if we argued at the dinner table, Luke would often form a "T" with his little hands and say, "Time out! Time out!" That's how inappropriate we could be.

We continued toward our destination in silence. Instead of commenting on God's marvelous creation surrounding us, we stared straight ahead and only spoke to one another when necessary. Upon arriving at the inn, we faked our smiles and tried to look happy for our exuberant *Christian* hostess, which only made things worse.

The rest of our weekend developed into a miserable series of hits and misses. Stu and I would make up and try to get along, but soon another issue would surface. I couldn't delight in the fact that Stu graciously brought coffee to me in bed both mornings or that he let me read my favorite magazines and nap to my heart's content. I had built up tremendous expectations for our weekend together—and of my husband—that couldn't possibly be met.

When our trip was over, instead of feeling rested and refreshed, I wished we'd never gone in the first place. In my mind, since we'd experienced conflict from the outset, the entire trip was a waste of time and money. Instead of focusing on the fun we had hiking to a huge antique waterwheel or appreciating the reproduction pitcher and basin Stu bought me, all I recalled were the harsh words and arguments.

Secret 1

Looking back, I realize our dream-weekend-gone-south was a turning point for me. As I spent time in prayer after the trip, God showed me how I often threw out the baby with the bath water. If Stu and I didn't get along perfectly, I completely dismissed whatever experience we had shared. You've heard the expression, "Do you see the glass as half-empty or half-full?" Well, with my temperament and personality, it wasn't only half-empty, there wasn't even any water in it! If you're like me and find that you need all the stars to line up emotionally before you can enjoy your husband, you need to know and apply this first secret to make your marriage sizzle: Let go of perfection.

Edith Schaeffer, in *Celebration of Marriage*, described it this way: "The decision was made to stop, try to recognize the total value of what was happening, and make a deliberate choice that the broken, torn, spilled, crushed, burned, scratched, smashed, spoiled thing was not as important as the person, the moment of history, or the memory...."[2]

In this passage, Mrs. Schaeffer referred to her only new dress, which was ruined by a ketchup spill at the first place she and her husband ate on their honeymoon. But I found myself applying this principle—making the choice *not* to focus on the temporary disappointment of the moment but rather on my relationship with my husband and what I longed for it to be.

The Big Letdown

Several years ago, a friend of mine told her husband she needed a Saturday off just to get her "mother battery" recharged. Laura was right in the middle of the "multiple children under six" syndrome and desperately needed a break. After a wonderful day of window shopping, buying a new blouse, and sharing a great lunch with her sister, Laura finally felt ready to resume her responsibilities as the twenty-four-hour-a-day, on-call wonder woman called mom.

Laura drove home with visions of a clean house and her husband playing outside with the children. She was sure they'd spent the morning at the park or at least on the swing set in the backyard, enjoying the fact that Dad could push them so much higher than Mom. Maybe they'd had lunch at the nearby McDonald's, which would be a real treat. Laura grew happier and happier as she approached her house, anticipating the excitement that awaited her as the children clamored to tell her all about their day with Dad.

When Laura walked through the front door, her bubble burst. It was three o'clock in the afternoon, and all three of her children still wore pajamas. A football game blared on the television, and crayons lay scattered across the carpet. The heartwarming reunion Laura had pictured turned into a freezing showdown with her husband in a matter of seconds.

"Thanks a lot!" Laura spewed, hands on her hips. "I leave for part of one day, and nothing gets done around here. You don't even get the kids dressed and ... and ... you're trying to squeeze in quality time during the time-outs of a football game!"

Laura's husband looked at her in shock, unsure of how to respond to this sputtering, angry stranger. She stormed to their bedroom for her own time-out. *Why am I acting like this?* she thought. *Why am I so upset with Mark? He never told me what he was going to do with the kids today. I should just be thankful he was so sweet about telling me to go and have a good time. He works hard, too, and didn't begrudge my having the day to myself.*

Then Laura remembered the article on how to be a good Christian father she'd read earlier in the week. It specifically mentioned that playing with the children when the clock stops running during a televised football game did not count as quality time. While the author had a good point, for Laura and her husband on this day, at this time, it was not helpful.

How often do we sabotage a special weekend together, a dinner out, or even a cozy night at home—exactly as Laura did—because of disappointment with our husbands? We mentally run through the list of everything they've done wrong or all the promises they've broken. He didn't get the oil changed in my car. He forgot to pick Stephanie up from volleyball practice. When I wanted to talk about the latest issue at work/church/women's ministry, he was so zoned out on the latest play-off game (do they *ever* end?), he just nodded and said, "That's nice, honey."

When we allow ourselves to think this way—comparing our husbands to the ideal men described in many well-meaning books and magazines—our guys just don't measure up. And when they're not ideal husbands, we figure we don't need to be ideal wives.

Bedroom Barriers

This emphasis on perfection and magnifying the dissatisfactions in our marriages can carry over to the physical relationship with our husbands.

As a child, I didn't have a Christian marriage modeled for me. After I got married, I read every book I could get my hands on that taught how to be a good Christian wife and what a Christian marriage should look like. From these authors I learned that it is important to have major and minor problems resolved before a husband and wife enjoy one another physically.

Well, guess what? I was such a perfectionist, I constantly put our sexual relationship on hold because I felt we needed to talk about and work out every problem. One of the aspects of letting go of perfection in your marriage is realizing things don't have to be perfect between you and your husband before you come together sexually. In fact, many times if you can lay aside an issue and simply celebrate the physical aspect of your relationship, it opens the door to good communication, especially for him.

> Many times if you can lay aside an issue and simply celebrate the physical aspect of your relationship, it opens the door to good communication, especially for him.

Genesis 2:24 reads, "For this reason a man will leave his father and mother and be united to his wife, and they will become one flesh." The interchange that takes place emotionally and spiritually between a man and woman when they come together physically in the act of marriage is such a profound mystery that the apostle Paul, in Ephesians 5:32, compared it to the relationship between Christ and the church.

Becoming one physically with your husband bonds the two of you together in a way nothing else can. Engaging in sex outside marriage brings brokenness and pain. It wounds our fragile hearts. But God intended for the sexual act within the bounds of marriage to actually bring healing to our wounded hearts, just as Jesus Christ brings healing to our wounded lives. The emotional closeness that occurs after sexual intercourse often creates a safe and intimate atmosphere to address problems.

Please understand that I am not advocating denial or the continual stuffing of painful emotions. Every marriage has its seasons of difficulties in which differences must be discussed. What I am suggesting is that every once in a while you put that persistent problem, that familiar pain, that recent irritation on the back burner and simply enjoy your husband. Many times I have found that after making love, the problem I thought was so glaring and important no longer existed. It had evaporated in the warmth of our time spent loving one another.

Even when you're faced with a complex or thorny issue that will not go away, you may find your husband is much more open to discussion and compromise after you make love. This is especially true if you haven't used your sexuality as a bartering chip, a favor to grant or withhold from him at your whim, depending on whether or not he is in your good graces at the time.

As women, we tend to do that, don't we? If we are unhappy with the way our husbands treat us or if we don't like his latest decision, we may withhold the very thing that will draw him closer to us and bind our hearts together.

If perfection is something you struggle with, I want to encourage you. Don't allow dissatisfaction and unmet expectations in your relationship to keep you and your husband from coming together sexually. This behavior will only drive a wedge between you and make both of you vulnerable to the Enemy and his attacks on your marriage. Nothing delights Satan more than bringing down and destroying marriages—especially those committed to Christ.

Ecclesiastes 11:4 (TLB) reminds us, "If you wait for perfect conditions, you will never get anything done." That's truth we could apply to many areas of our lives, but it's especially appropriate if we want to raise the temperature in our marriages from lukewarm to sizzle!

Several years after I began teaching on how letting go of perfection increases romance and passion in marriage, I found a magazine article titled "Women That Men Love." Since I'm always on the lookout for information related to my talks, I eagerly read through the eight descriptions listed. Point six stated, "Women that men love don't have to have the perfect romantic atmosphere, perfect conditions, or even the perfect moment in the relationship to enjoy having sex with their mate."[3] Wow! I felt I'd hit the mark!

High-Maintenance Marriage

Lowering your expectations and letting go of perfection may be particularly hard if you have what I call a high-maintenance marriage. These relationships require large amounts of effort, focus, and attention. How do you know if you are in such a marriage? Answer the following questions: Are you often emotionally exhausted and spent? Do you have a depressing sense of hopelessness that your marriage will never really change for the better? Do you believe that no matter how hard you try, whatever you do is never enough or is never good enough for your spouse? Do you experience high moments of hope and joy followed by deep valleys of sorrow and despair? If you answered yes to several of these questions, you are in a high-maintenance marriage.

Several factors contribute to these special marriages. Some may be situational, such as issues related to jobs, housing arrangements, the number and ages of the children, and especially finances. Personality and temperament may also play a part in the high-maintenance marriage. If either you or your spouse has a phlegmatic temperament, you probably won't find yourself in this type of marriage, because phlegmatics tend to be peace loving and easygoing. These comfortable partners would rather defer to someone else's wishes than get into a confrontation over the many issues that arise in a marriage. It just isn't worth the hassle to them.[4]

Finally, another important element of high-maintenance marriages can stem from a spouse's childhood and family background. Learned attitudes and behaviors, particularly inappropriate ones, and any abuse that was present add to a person's makeup.

Every one of these elements—circumstances, temperament, and upbringing—may determine whether your marriage is high or low maintenance. If either you or your spouse came from a difficult family, I can't emphasize enough the value Christian counseling or support groups can lend to bringing you healing and wholeness, as well as to your marriage. Proverbs 24:6 (NASB) promises, "In abundance of counselors there is victory." My prayer is that you will experience the victory the Lord desires in your marriage, especially if it is a high-maintenance one.

Recently I spoke with a woman who was in such a marriage. We didn't know each other very well, but it was one of those conversations that went from zero to sixty in record time. In fact, her husband was sitting right next to her when she shared, "The first ten years we were married, I didn't even like being married, especially to him!"

I was mortified for her husband's sake, but he just smiled. Obviously, he'd heard this before. Now, this Christian couple had dated several years before they married. But the reality of marriage was just a little more than this wife could handle at the time.

As we talked, I asked her, "What kept you together those first ten years?"

She replied, "Our sex life. It was great!"

I told her that was a clear mercy of God. When you are intimate physically, you make yourself vulnerable, which helps keep the emotional barriers down.

The First Step

As wives, how can we begin to lower our expectations of our husbands and release them from needing to perform perfectly in order to gain our love? The first and most essential step in becoming the loving, accepting wife your husband will adore is *prayer*. Have you ever noticed you can talk to your husband over and over about the same topic? You can cry, explain, nag, or even beg, but things still stay the same, even though the desire for change is there. Yet, that same amount of energy, if invested in prayer, can yield tremendous results and lasting change. Stormie Omartian wrote in *The Power of a Praying Wife*, "I lay all my expectations at your cross. I release my husband from the burden of fulfilling me in areas where I should be looking to you.... Only you, Lord, are perfect and I look to you to perfect us."5

> Let the Lord lead you in how to pray for him, and let God be the one to bring about any necessary changes in your marriage.

Ladies, let your husbands go! Let the Lord lead you in how to pray for him, and let God be the one to bring about any necessary changes in your marriage.

Agreeably Adapting

A second important step toward lowering your expectations of your husband is learning to *submit* to him as God's chosen leader in your home. I have always liked the way J. B. Phillips translated Ephesians 5:22–23 in the *New Testament in Modern English*: "You wives must learn to adapt yourselves to your husbands, as you submit yourselves to the Lord, for the husband is the 'head' of the wife in the same way that Christ is the head of the Church and saviour of his Body."

The word *adapt* presents an attractive picture of what our relationships to our husbands can be. It means to "make fit or suitable by changing or adjusting oneself, *especially* (my emphasis) to new or changed circumstances."[6] It also implies flexibility.

My good friend Tina lived out this principle so beautifully before my eyes. She and I have known each other since childhood. Her family belonged to a legalistic denomination and her upbringing was very strict. When she married John, who had only recently committed his life to the Lord, I was sure sparks would fly because John didn't think anything was wrong with drinking alcohol. Also, as a new Christian, he didn't know the principle of tithing. Many other practices that came second nature to Tina, John just had never heard about.

Soon after their wedding, Tina invited Stu and me to their home for dinner. Their perfectly appointed dining room gleamed with fine bone china, a lace tablecloth, matching linen napkins, and even Tina's sterling silver and crystal wine glasses. When John brought out a bottle of red wine, uncorked it, and poured Tina half a glass, I almost fell off my chair. She acted like nothing was out of the ordinary and lifted her glass in a toast to our first dinner together in their home.

Later, I pulled Tina aside and quietly asked her, "When did you start drinking wine? What will your parents say?"

"Denise, John and I have talked about this at length, and I realized I don't want one little glass of wine to be a stumbling block in our marriage. I've already told my parents that John drinks wine once in a while with dinner, but out of respect for them, he won't do so when they come to visit or stay with us."

Tina applied this same principle to the issue of tithing. As a lawyer, John earns a very good income. Once they married, Tina believed they should give a tenth of his salary to their local church. Again, Tina calmly discussed with John what it means to tithe, and he agreed to think about it. She then let the subject drop and patiently prayed that God would begin to work in John's heart regarding honoring the Lord with their finances.

> This is one of the hardest things to do, isn't it? Share our perspectives with our husbands and then release them (both our perspectives and our husbands!) to the Lord.

A few weeks later, John said, "I've been thinking about our talk, and I've looked up the verses you mentioned on tithing. I feel God is asking me to give ten percent of our income to our church." Tina was very excited God answered her prayers so quickly, but I'm convinced a large part of this swift answer to prayer was Tina's willingness to let go of her expectations and let God be the one to change John's heart. Tina didn't withhold her love or support of John. Instead, after sharing her viewpoint, she took her concerns to the Lord in prayer and continued to behave with warmth and acceptance toward her husband.

This is one of the hardest things to do, isn't it? Share our perspectives with our husbands and then release them (both our perspectives and our husbands!) to the Lord. Even as I write this, I am convicted of different areas in my own marriage where I apply pressure—sometimes subtly and sometimes not so subtly—to get Stu to change his behavior and act how I think he should. The book of Proverbs refers to this as a "constant dripping" (19:13). In other words, a form of slow torture! And the only thing a constant drip in the home succeeds in doing is to drive everyone crazy.

The Forgiveness Factor

Let's look at an alternate ending to the story of Tina and John. What if, after their discussions and Tina's unconditional love, John had refused to tithe? Or, what if he acted in other ways that were detrimental to their new marriage? What could Tina have done then?

> Forgiveness is the oil that keeps the inner workings of a marriage running smoothly. Anger melts in the face of forgiveness, and forgiveness washes bitterness out of our souls.

Maybe you're more familiar with broken promises, unmet needs, and daily disappointments than answered prayers and dreams come true. If so, the third and very necessary step you will need to take to release your husband from your expectations is *forgiveness*.

Ephesians 4:32 exhorts us to "Be kind and compassionate to

one another, forgiving each other, just as in Christ God forgave you." And even more serious, Mark 11:25 (NASB) warns us, "Whenever you stand praying, forgive, if you have anything against anyone; so that your Father who is in heaven will also forgive you your transgressions."

In other words, when we refuse to forgive, God will not forgive us. That's a sobering truth. One of the ways God shows His kindness and compassion to us is through His merciful forgiveness, and He asks us to do the same with our husbands.

Forgiveness is the oil that keeps the inner workings of a marriage running smoothly. Anger melts in the face of forgiveness, and forgiveness washes bitterness out of our souls. But when we refuse to forgive, little irritations get blown out of proportion and the smallest slights turn into serious hurts. Where forgiveness is lacking, bricks of offense lay a foundation for walls of anger and indifference. The higher and thicker these walls become, the more difficult they are to breach.

Perhaps the hardest aspect of forgiveness is getting past this line of thinking: *If I forgive my husband for _____, I'm letting him off the hook! He won't realize what he did was wrong and that he needs to change.* When you forgive your husband, you aren't saying what he did was right or condoning his bad behavior—you are simply obeying God's Word and making yourself pleasing to the Lord.

The next time your husband offends you, try this: First, go to God and ask Him aloud to help you forgive your husband for whatever he did that hurt you. Then, find a time to talk about the issue, preferably when little ones are in bed and big kids are doing their homework. This is not dinner-table conversation.

Next, without accusing or yelling, tell him what disappointed, angered, or wounded you. The best-case scenario is that he understands what you're saying and sincerely asks your forgiveness. However, this is one of those situations in marriage in which you may have to lower your expectations. If your husband listens to you but doesn't agree with what you've said or he agrees but isn't sorry, it may help for you to politely ask him to repeat what he thought you said. This communication technique ensures you've communicated clearly and he understands your point.

If, after all is said and done, you are still unable to reach an agreement or resolve the issue, quietly reassure your husband of your love and give him time to process what you've shared. Men don't always work through problems as quickly as women do. Even though my husband and I have been married for years, just a few months ago he reminded me, "I wish you wouldn't get upset with me when I don't see an issue from your point of view as soon as you share with me. I need time to process what you've said, especially if you're telling me I've hurt you." He's right!

> Living in forgiveness frees your heart to receive God's work on your behalf.

What if you can't forgive your husband? Once when Stu and I had both been deeply hurt by others regarding a situation at his job, I told the Lord, "God, I can't forgive these men. It's impossible. I know You want me to, and I wish I could do it, Jesus, but I can't." In that moment, the Lord gave me a powerful but simple answer: "Forgive them for My sake. Do this for Me. Don't do it for them, but do it for Me because I'm asking you to."

The Lord then showed me a prayer I've used many times when it seemed impossible to forgive Stu or someone else:

> Dear Jesus,
>
>   I forgive _____ for Your name's sake. I do this for

You, Lord, because You so graciously forgive me and because You ask me to. I want to be pleasing to You. I pray You will honor my desire to be obedient and bring whatever restoration between us that You desire. Amen.

Living in forgiveness frees your heart to receive God's work on your behalf. I have heard stories time and again of wives whose deepest desires were fulfilled *after* they forgave their husbands.

Perfect Praise

The fourth and final step to release your husband from your expectations and to let go of perfection in your marriage is *praise*. I want you to compliment him and show your appreciation for who he is and what he does. After all, these reasons are why you fell in love with him in the first place! But more importantly, take time every day, especially if you are struggling with loving and accepting your husband, to thank and praise God for your husband and for your marriage.

A woman from our weekly Bible study hit an all-time low in her high-maintenance marriage. Mary and her husband had sought Christian counseling because they both realized how much their marriage and love for one another had deteriorated. She had tried to be submissive and adaptable in most areas, but her husband was emotionally unstable due to trauma he had endured

> Take time every day, especially if you are struggling with loving and accepting your husband, to thank and praise God for your husband and for your marriage.

in childhood. This dear wife had forgiven her husband more times than we could count, and she felt that she went far beyond the "seventy times seven" Jesus spoke of in the Gospels. But still, her husband constantly talked about leaving her and the children.

They had planned one more night away as a "last chance" for their marriage. Her husband told her that if things didn't go better between them on this weekend, he was going to move out. About two weeks before their time away, several members of our Bible study group began discussing how thanking and praising God for specific hardships He allowed had made a difference in their situations. Their conviction was based on 1 Thessalonians 5:16–18: "Be joyful always; pray continually; *give thanks in all circumstances*, for this is God's will for you in Christ Jesus."

The next morning, as Mary desperately prayed for their marriage and family, the Lord prompted her: "Mary, you have never praised Me in the midst of these troubles. You have never thanked Me for these problems. Do you think all that is happening with Richard has escaped My notice? I want your praise."

First, Mary dusted off some praise CDs that she hadn't played for several months. She sang along with the choruses, praising and worshipping God as she went about her household chores. After a couple days of doing this, Mary began to thank God specifically for everything she could think of regarding her husband. Her prayers went something like this: "Lord, thank You that I loved Richard so much when we got married. Thank You that there was no one else for either of us, that we only wanted to marry each other. Thank You that Richard has been a Christian since he was a child. Thank You that even in the midst of our worst struggles, he has been faithful to take the children and me to church every week, even when I didn't want to go." Mary's prayers of thankfulness flowed on and on. Every day, after she worshipped the Lord with Christian music, she found new things to thank God for regarding Richard.

Just two days before Mary and Richard were to leave for their weekend, Mary had a tremendous change of heart. Again, she was thanking God for the positive aspects of their relationship, when God asked her, "Mary, what if I told you your number one ministry in life—even more important to Me than any other work you do at church or for others—is to help bring healing and wholeness to your husband?"

Mary confessed to our group that if God had asked this before her time of praising Him and thanking Him, she probably couldn't have accepted those words. But because she had set her will to praise God for her husband and her marriage, and because God met her not just spiritually but emotionally, Mary said yes to God's request.

Richard responded to Mary's change of heart with tears in his eyes. He admitted he was the major source of their problems, and vowed to work on his character. Richard told her he felt God resurrected their marriage that weekend. All this happened more than two years ago. They are still together, doing better than ever. He never moved out.

"A good marriage is not one where perfection reigns; it is a relationship where a healthy perspective overlooks a multitude of 'unresolvables.'"[7]

LANGUAGE OF LOVERS

... each one heard them speaking in his [or her] own language.

Acts 2:6

Have you ever traveled to a foreign country and not known the language? Last summer I had the privilege of traveling to Italy for the first time. Students from our church taught free English camps, and I was fortunate enough to be one of the adult chaperones. Even though most of the Italians we came in contact with knew a little English, communication was still difficult. By the end of each day, our heads spun with the effort it took to initiate and maintain conversations. In fact, one miscommunication due to the language barrier stranded a group of us by a lake until ten o'clock one night!

Two of our church students, however, didn't struggle like the rest of us. Mike studied Italian for more than two months before we left, and Sarah naturally became fluent in Italian once we arrived. These teens proved invaluable on our trip. Sarah and Mike made all the Italians we met feel special and important because these two Americans cared enough to learn the language.

At every class we taught, we asked the attendees *why* they were interested in learning English. They gave several answers. "English is the language of business"; "English is the language of money"; "English is the language of the world." If English is the language of the world, then love is *the* language for marriage and close relationships. And just as English is spoken differently in various regions of the United States, love is spoken and understood in diverse ways. Furthermore, *not* knowing this method of communication can make the love relationship with your spouse as frustrating as trying to get your needs met in a foreign country where neither of you understands or speaks the language of the other.

Secret 2

Stu and I first heard about the "five love languages"[1] in a Sunday school class more than fifteen years ago. Norm Evans, formerly of the Miami Dolphins, and his wife, Bobbi, taught the principles that became a huge turning point in our marriage. Since then, author Gary Chapman has written a series of books describing in depth the five love languages and how to apply them to your closest relationships. I like to include a discussion of the love languages in all of my "Sizzle" talks, because in every group several women have never heard of them.

> Spouses who learn their partner's language and "speak" it regularly maximize the feelings of love we all want to experience in our marriages.

If you already know the love languages, you may want to skim over this chapter as a quick refresher course. Sometimes we forget how beneficial an idea is until we're once again reminded of it. But if you've never heard of the five love languages, you're in for a treat. Spouses who learn their partner's language and "speak" it regularly maximize the feelings of love we all want to experience in our marriages. With these thoughts in mind, the second secret to making your marriage sizzle and to increasing emotional intimacy is to learn one another's love language and speak it as often as possible.

Each of us has a primary and secondary pathway or language of giving and receiving love. For instance, you may show your husband he is loved by making his lunch every morning before he leaves for work.

We also tend to express love to our spouses and others in the manner in which we like to receive it.

We also tend to express love to our spouses and others in the manner in which we like to receive it. We do this because we assume that since a certain action or attitude would make us feel loved, it will make our spouses or others feel loved as well. However, husbands and wives often don't speak the same love language (are we surprised?). He makes sure your tires are rotated and the oil gets changed in your car, while you would prefer a dozen coral roses wrapped in a salmon-colored bow. You tell him "I love you" every day, while he would prefer that you make love more often. These common miscues often leave us feeling hurt and uncared for, unless, by chance, you and your husband are fortunate enough to share the same love language.

Recognizing and practicing the five love languages has the potential to improve all of your relationships because others will feel more loved and cared for when you learn and speak their primary love language to them.

An Important Question

I'm always asked, "How can I tell which language is really mine or my husband's?" If, after reading through the descriptions of the five love languages, you can't decide which one describes you best, keep this in mind: You will most likely feel unloved and taken for granted when your primary and/or secondary love languages are not spoken, even if your spouse is showing love to you in other ways.

With this in mind, pay attention over the next few weeks. See if your "love tank" is full to overflowing based on your husband's words and actions toward you, or if it feels awfully close to empty. And, if your husband isn't sure what his primary love language is, try different expressions of love from each category. Then ask him every few days if he feels highly valued or not.

Apples of Gold: The Language of Affirming Words

Throughout the ages, men and women have wooed and declared their undying love through words. Elizabeth Barrett Browning and her husband, Robert Browning, courted and won one another's affection, which led to an extremely romantic marriage where passion glowed undimmed over the years through their words. Proverbs 25:11 (AB) tells us, "A word fitly spoken and in due season is like apples of gold in settings of silver." The right words spoken at the right time are beautiful to hear and uplift our souls.

Sincere compliments and verbal affirmations of love and respect remain just as powerful today. Whether or not we realize it, words have the ability to provide a great deal of emotional security to some of us.

Are you a woman who likes to hear, "Honey, you look great in that outfit"? Or, "I really like the way you did your hair today"? Or my all-time favorite, "Have I told you lately how much I love you?" If one of your love languages is words, your heart is singing right about now! You know how much praise and positive words mean to you.

In our home, my husband likes to give words and I like to receive them. He's a salesman and I'm an author/speaker, so he is used to giving words to connect with a customer, and I am wired to respond to words. Verbal affirmation is my secondary love language, and for years my husband has blessed me by giving me loving words every morning with my coffee.

Now, please don't get jealous when I tell you that for most of our married life my husband has brought me my coffee in bed each morning. This wonderful tradition began when we had our babies. A little one would wake up around 5:30 or 6:00 a.m. (you know how they do), and my husband soon realized I was practically incapable of feeding them, changing their diapers, and so forth without a good, strong cup of coffee. He found that if he brought the baby, the diaper, the bottle, and the coffee to me at the same time, everyone got taken care of, and he could get on with his day.

Even though our babies are now grown, Stu still strolls into our room (he is definitely a morning person), steaming mug of coffee in hand. As he sets it on the nightstand beside me, he offers a comment like "Good morning, beautiful!" Ironically, my face is usually buried in a pillow when he greets me, so he is talking to the back of my head. Suffice it to say, I know my husband isn't

> One way you can tell if you are speaking your spouse's love language is that he will light up right before your eyes when his language is spoken.

being quite truthful when he calls me "beautiful" in the morning, but I don't care. It's a great way for a "words" woman like me to start the day.

But perhaps your husband is the words person around your house. If so, try this little experiment when he comes home tonight. When you have his attention, give him a compliment. Tell him how much you appreciate how hard he works for you and the kids, or say you noticed how handsome he looked in his suit (or work shirt or whatever!) when he walked through the door.

One way you can tell if you are speaking your spouse's love language is that he will light up right before your eyes when his language is spoken. As an aside (and most of you probably already know this), men like to be praised in *manly* ways, not with cutesy phrases. Compliment your man on his muscles, how he takes care of your family, his wisdom in a decision at work, or even his sexual prowess in bed (he'll really like that one!)—anything that emphasizes his role as provider, protector, and knight in shining armor for you and your family. Telling him how much it meant to you that he loaded his own dishes into the dishwasher that morning might not cause him to light up—even if words are his primary love language.

> People whose primary love language is words can be easily crushed by hurtful or thoughtless comments.

Several things could happen when you try this experiment: (a) he passes out because it's been so long since he heard a compliment (I *know* this won't be true); (b) he looks at you funny, shrugs his shoulders, and says in a slightly monotone voice, "Oh"; or (c) he lights up like a Christmas tree and goes through the rest of the night with a merry glow on his face. If the response you get is C, it's probable that one of your husband's love languages is words.

Sticks and Stones

A crucial point to remember about people whose love language is words is they can be sensitive to negative words, especially if those words are directed toward them. People whose primary love language is words can be easily crushed by hurtful or thoughtless comments. These individuals often take things literally or at face value. Jokes may pass them right by, and sarcasm will wound them. It's no surprise they don't respond well to verbal brow beating or criticism not softened by praise.

> Hurtful words sting, and their aftereffects can be felt for a lifetime.

As grown-ups, we know the familiar children's jingle "Sticks and stones may break my bones, but words will never hurt me" simply isn't true. Hurtful words sting, and their aftereffects can be felt for a lifetime. Proverbs 18:21 (NASB) strongly states, "Death and life are in the power of the tongue." In other words, we can speak in a way that kills someone's spirit or brings others to life.

In Dr. Laura Schlessinger's book *The Proper Care and Feeding of Husbands*, she gives an example of one husband's response to his wife's hypercriticism over how he did the dishes. (Wouldn't most of us be tickled pink if our guys helped us in the kitchen?) Petrified she would find yet another mistake to condemn him for, this man stood at the kitchen sink with tears streaming down his face—at which point his wife yelled, "I want a divorce. I have to do everything anyway!"[2] This is a tragic example of words used as a sword and inflicting great pain.

Perhaps women in particular struggle with what comes out of our mouths. I know I certainly do. The most frequent sin I ask the Lord's forgiveness for is something I've said during the course of my day. Either I said something out of line or in an inappropriate tone.

The root of our problem may lie in the fact that women need to speak about twenty-five thousand words a day to feel satisfied, while men require only ten thousand words. Just the sheer volume of words we need to use every day leaves us susceptible to misusing them. Proverbs warns us, "When words are many, sin is not absent" (10:19). That dooms so many of us to failure right there!

One of my favorite quotes is from the fictional character Father Tim of the Mitford series by Jan Karon. In describing his mother, Tim said, "She was a highly verbal woman who also knew the priceless value of being quiet."[3] If we are unsure of what to say in a situation, it usually doesn't hurt to keep quiet. In addition, when we're extremely angry, it's probably best not to give full vent to our feelings of the moment. And, on those rare occasions when I find myself at a loss for words, instead of feeling frustrated, I remind myself, "Even a fool is thought wise if [s]he keeps silent" (Prov. 17:28).

My Favorite Language: Gifts

The language of gifts is my favorite love language. For years my husband thought I was a little greedy because I often asked for presents. What neither of us understood at the time was that I needed concrete evidence of his love for me. If you or someone you love has the love language of gifts, it doesn't mean you or he is necessarily materialistic, because a gift doesn't need to be expensive to be appreciated by the "gifts" person. If your love language is gifts, the reason you feel loved when your husband gives you a present is because it means he was thinking of you.

My friend Catherine has a sweet husband who knows her primary love language is gifts. Marv likes to satisfy her craving for frozen yogurt by bringing home the "flavor of the month," complete with her favorite toppings. He also spoke her love language in a big way for her fiftieth birthday with a surprise trip on a chartered sailboat with four of their best friends! What really makes this special is Marv would have preferred having Catherine all to himself; however, he knew she would enjoy their friends' company.

An A+ Student

Until Stu and I learned about love languages, I would scrimp and save to buy him a new shirt or pair of pants. (Did I mention I love clothes? Who was I thinking of here, really?) All day I'd anticipate his surprise and delight that I'd carved out the time and money to buy him some new clothes. *Wrong!* He would look at the shirt or pants or whatever I'd laid out on the bed and say, "That's nice," in an unemotional way. Needless to say, I was crushed and couldn't understand why he wasn't more excited. I certainly would have been.

After we learned my love language was gifts, Stu understood for the first time why gifts, or tangible expressions of his love, were so important to me. Fortunately, I'm married to a fast learner. First, fresh strawberries accompanied my morning coffee. Then he did something that showed he really understood what the language of gifts is all about.

When our children were small, the television show *Thirtysomething* was popular. Since we fell in that age group, I could often relate to the situations portrayed. Stu, however, did not share my enthusiasm. He felt it was a "chick" show and usually found something else to do when it aired.

Even though he didn't care to watch it, Stu did feel sorry for me when the program was canceled. On the Tuesday night before the final episode aired, he was helping me clean up after dinner. All of a sudden he said, "I forgot something in the van today. It's on the passenger side. Could you go get it for me?"

When I opened the passenger door of our van, there, folded neatly on the seat, was a purple cotton nightshirt from a local department store with "thirtysomething" in bold print across the front.

I ran in to the house so excited! While I was thanking him, Stu said, "I knew the last show was tonight, and I wanted you to be able to wear that nightshirt while you were watching it." Did he get it or what?

The other thing you need to know about Stu is that he is a man who does not shop. Once a year he will go to a store with me to buy clothes for him, but usually I just pick them out. For Stu to actually take the time to go to the store and buy me that nightshirt (and it wasn't even sexy!) was equivalent to my trying to find just the right drill bit in Home Depot! This gesture spoke volumes to me of his loving care and thoughtfulness.

The love language of gifts can be spoken even without a big budget. The key is to be sensitive and listen for the little things that would brighten your man's day.

Tips on Gift Giving

Now before you get dismayed because your

husband can't give you a trip to the Caribbean or you can't buy him tickets to the Super Bowl, be encouraged. The love language of gifts can be spoken even without a big budget. The key is to be sensitive and listen for the little things that would brighten your man's day. Try to find out the title of a book he would like to read or the latest CD he'd like to get. Maybe he's been eyeing a new gadget for the garage that you could save up for and surprise him with. A friend of ours, Peter, is a "bagaholic." He collects every kind of bag you can think of: backpacks, fanny packs, notebook carriers, and several types of briefcases. If he were a woman, he'd have a closet full of purses! So his wife, Maggie, is always on the lookout for different or unusual bags at flea markets or garage sales. Gift giving can be done even on a shoestring.

If you're the gifts person, make a list of the little things that would make you feel loved. Keep it short if money is tight. Instead of getting depressed that you have to list presents you'd appreciate, it's best to realize that if your husband is not a gifts person, it may be hard for him to recall what you'd like to receive. Remember, the delight will lie in which one he'll pick, and the joy of surprise comes when he gives it to you. (If you are both gifts people, you may want to hide the credit cards!)

Furthermore, it's usually not much fun for the person whose love language is gifts to get something he or she actually needs. This might be all right once in a while, but definitely not on a regular basis. For instance, if your husband is trying to speak your love language and decides to get you a toaster, you may not feel very excited. Practical presents are useful, but they probably won't light the romantic fires like a yummy box of chocolates.

Finally, Proverbs reminds us, "A gift opens the way for the giver" (18:16). If you've had a spat with your husband, family member, or close friend—and he or she is a gifts person—go shopping! Even a well-chosen greeting card can help smooth things over. And if you're the gifts person, a peace offering can soften the hardest of hearts.

Love in Action: The Language of Serving

Everyone knows the old saying, "Actions speak louder than words." To the woman whose love language is serving, her heart cry would be, "Don't just say you love me, *show* me!" Most acts of service are made up of the tasks and chores of everyday life. Cooking a meal, washing the dishes, vacuuming, taking out the garbage, mowing the lawn, or putting gas in the car are all examples of this love language. When common duties are done with the welfare of your spouse in mind, you communicate love in a powerful way.

> When common duties are done with the welfare of your spouse in mind, you communicate love in a powerful way.

The Bible clearly tells us the high value of showing love through what we do: "Dear children, let us not love with words or tongue but with actions and in truth" (1 John 3:18). For many men, the love language of serving is the primary way they express love to their wives and families. When a wife sincerely questions her husband's love for her because he rarely says I love you, a man with the love language of serving replies, "Of course I love you! I work hard for our family, I take care of the cars, I do all of the yard work. Do you think I do these things for myself?" Unfortunately, due to the feminization of our culture and the expectation that men should get in touch with their feelings and express their emotions like women do, this valid love language has been minimized and even dismissed.

Does your husband fall into this category? Is he the hard-working, stoic provider who shoulders much of the responsibility in your home? Instead of criticizing him for not being as verbal as you'd like, why not try thanking God—and him—for taking seriously his role as protector and provider? He will probably feel deeply appreciated and relieved that you are able to sense his love for you when he has been trying so hard.

It might be tempting to think, *But aren't these responsibilities we all have to do? How can rotating the tires on my car be a love language?* When women think of love, we tend to think only of romance—heartfelt poetry, sentimental cards, beautiful flowers, or expensive candlelight dinners. All of these lovely demonstrations make us feel special.

But have you ever been seriously ill? Or maybe you're just overwhelmed by the never-ending demands of small children. If so, you know firsthand how meaningful a cheery, "Don't worry, honey; I'll bathe the kids and tuck them in tonight" can be. In fact, I meet women all the time who tell me their primary love language is serving. They have sweet, fun-loving husbands but would give anything for their guys to come home from work and offer to cook dinner or clean up the kitchen so they can have a break. I encourage these overworked women to make it worth their husbands' while. Put your arms around his neck, give him a kiss, and let him know you'll save the extra energy you'll have from your break for him.

Perhaps you've realized your primary or secondary love language is serving. You would rather have your husband mop the kitchen floor than buy you an expensive but unnecessary gift. Perhaps it would mean more to you if he took out the garbage without your reminding him than if he told you how beautiful you look for the hundredth time that day. But how can you tell if acts of service would make your husband feel loved?

If one of your husband's love languages is serving, he'll be grateful for the wonderful, or even not so wonderful (corndogs, maybe?), meals you've prepared. He'll love having his laundry done so he doesn't run out of the clothes he needs. He'll like your home to be picked up and in order. And you'll really score points if you sewed the button onto his shirt that's been off for months. You see, he needs signs of physical tasks you've done throughout the day to show you care for him and your family.

A friend and her husband lived a good lifestyle, so she routinely sent his shirts out to be laundered, starched, and ironed. But Bill always complained about this, and Cheryl didn't understand why. When Cheryl and Bill learned about the love languages, they both realized service was important for him, which was why he didn't feel taken care of when she sent his shirts to the cleaners.

Another woman asked her husband what she could do to show her love for him. She was sure he'd respond with some wild suggestion about their sex life, which would have been fine with her. Instead, he replied, "I'd love it if you made my lunch in the morning for me." This smart wife went to the nearest deli and stocked up on his favorite lunchmeats and cheeses. He, in turn, rewarded her with more of the physical intimacy she longed for.

> So much of our lives as women is spent taking care of others that when our husbands make the effort to take care of us we feel loved, cherished, and understood.

Icing on the Cake

Finally, the love language of serving also includes the chivalrous way a man treats his wife, such as opening the car door for her, taking her elbow when crossing the street, or arranging all the details for a special date together. Old-fashioned manners like these never go out of style and are especially meaningful to a woman whose love language is service. So much of our lives as women is spent taking care of others that when our husbands make the effort to take care of us we feel loved, cherished, and understood. The fires of romance are lit, and our hearts are warmed with a little tender loving care.

One of the delicate responsibilities we have as wives is to lovingly help our husbands understand how much this romantic attention means to us. It is the bridge that smoothes over the troubled waters of a difficult marriage and the icing on the marriage that is sometimes a bit crumbly. So don't give up if your husband doesn't get it at first. Just keep letting him know what a great wife and sizzling love life are in store for him!

A Note of Caution

Here's a quick note for all wives on the language of service. I have met many couples in which the husband works hard to support his family so the wife is able to stay at home. However, she doesn't always use her time wisely to keep things running smoothly for him and the family. One husband often told me that he felt taken advantage of. If this is true in your home, I pray you will correct matters. Playing several days a week while your husband works isn't right or fair. Amy Dacyczyn—author of *The Tightwad Gazette*, a practical manual on money-saving ideas for the home—wrote, "Whichever spouse stays at home should put in the same amount of working hours each day that the spouse going to a job does."[4]

Now, I'm the first to admit my husband works much longer and harder days than I do. He is physically stronger than I am and able to bear it. First Peter 3:7 (KJV) reminds men to live with their wives in an understanding way as with a "weaker vessel."

Husbands are to recognize that most women don't have the same amount of physical strength and stamina as men. However, this doesn't give us license to play the day away and take for granted a good husband's strong work ethic. You're likely to end up with a cranky, resentful husband if you do. Remember to treat others as you would like to be treated.

One wife who liked to play a lot had a rude awakening when her husband lost his job, and she had to return to work. She arrived home each night at the dinner hour to find no dinner started, the house a mess, and kids waiting to be picked up from sports practice or shuttled to piano lessons. After a few weeks, she humbly confessed to our Bible study, "I see what Roger meant all those years. The shoe is on the other foot now."

Now I know there are wives who work hard each day to take care of the children and home. Yet, when their husband arrives home from work, he feels he has put in his time for the day and shouldn't have to do anything else. This attitude can be discouraging to a worn-out wife, especially if she has young children. If this is true for you, try gently suggesting your relationship will become better if he pitches in occasionally because you'll have more time and energy for each other. When the work is evenly divided, everyone benefits.

Love Is Spelled T-I-M-E: The Language of Quality Time

If your husband's love language is meaningful time, you will never be a lonely wife. Why? Because your man won't feel satisfied unless he emotionally connects with you for at least fifteen to twenty minutes every day, and he will often just want to be with you. One definition of quality time is giving a spouse, child, or friend your undivided attention while you listen to what is said and then respond with thoughtfulness. Your beloved knows you are totally "present" with him in the moment. No matter how crazy this husband's day was, he'll want to check in with you and talk before the night is over.

The meaningful-time husband shows genuine interest in his wife and her day. He will often ask, "Did you see any of your friends today?" "How are the kids? Are there any problems?" "Is everything okay with you?" or the perennial favorite, "Is there anything I can pray about for you?" In return, this husband needs you to ask him thoughtful questions and to track with his answers. Channel surfing or working on your

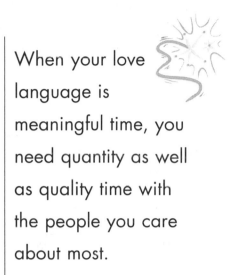

When your love language is meaningful time, you need quantity as well as quality time with the people you care about most.

latest cross-stitch project while your mate is trying to talk does not go over well when your love language is meaningful time. You feel rejected if you have only half of your mate's attention during a conversation. One wife told us the television has to be off and she can't be looking at a magazine when her husband is ready for their talk time in bed.

The love language of time is also simply being together. One dear husband we know often asks his wife to go with him to his shop while he works on their boat just so they can be together. Large amounts of time spent together can turn even everyday moments into quality time. When your love language is meaningful time, you need quantity as well as quality time with the people you care about most.

As you might have guessed, the meaningful-time husband is almost every woman's dream. Date nights are a priority as well as talking on the phone during the day. However, the language of serving is a common way for men to express their love, which may reduce meaningful time with their wives. For this reason, quality time is the love language many women still need to hear to feel affirmed and loved by their husbands.

Quality time is the primary love language of our daughter, Brynne. Ever since she was little, she would wander through the house to find me, grab my hand, and ask, "Mommy, when are we going to be a family?" I knew she meant when would we all be together in the same room, talking, laughing, and having fun. Even as a teenager, this precious daughter will often run home for lunch just to be with me if she knows she isn't going to see me that evening. For Brynne, love is spelled T-I-M-E.

Honey, Are You Listening?

One of the greatest complaints women have toward men in general is "He never listens to me!" For the wife whose love language is meaningful time, this can be a cause for deep hurt instead of merely irritation. I believe part of many men's seeming inability to listen is due to the fact that most men are visual or kinesthetic learners and processors who primarily respond to their environments through sight or activity. Listening, however, involves auditory processing, receiving information through hearing.

When Darla and Ken were dating, she thought she'd found the ideal man. Every afternoon they'd meet on the lawn of their college campus for lunch. As Darla talked, Ken would look at her intently, incline his head, and say "uh-huh" and "ummm" every so often. After they married, Darla learned the truth during a routine conversation with Ken.

"So what do you think?" she asked him.

He blinked a moment in surprise and turned red.

"Ken," she persisted, "what did I just say?"

Embarrassed, he shrugged his shoulders and replied, "I don't know!"

Darla realized Ken had never been truly interested in what she had to say; he was instead giving Darla his "salesman glaze." Because he was in sales, customers would talk at length about their lives, problems, or families. In order to cope, Ken had learned to tune out by nodding once in a while and making small sounds of agreement.

If your husband is listening challenged like Ken, you might want to try some of the following suggestions to ensure he stays with you when you're talking.

- Keep your sentences simple, brief, and to the point. For example, say, "Music practice went really well tonight" instead of "Music practice was great tonight. At first I couldn't get the song right, so Mike, the worship leader, told me to try ... blah, blah, blah." You know what I mean. Give your husband the *Reader's Digest Condensed Version* and save the full-length novel for your girlfriends.

- Limit yourself to three topics at one sitting. Decide throughout the day what three things are the most important to tell your husband. If you get through talking in less than ten minutes and you want to bring up other subjects, go ahead. Just pay attention to his body language and quit talking if you are losing him; he will appreciate your sensitivity, and you will avoid getting your feelings hurt.

- Include questions that can't be answered with a simple yes or no throughout your conversation to draw him in. Ask him, "What do you think about ...?" or "How would you handle ...?"

- If you'd like an indication he has heard what you said and aren't looking for him to fix any problems for you, let him know these phrases speak your love language: "I'm sorry, honey. That must have hurt you."

"I'm glad you enjoyed yourself so much!"

"You must have felt good about that."

"Would you like to pray about it?"

Given at the appropriate time, any of these responses will go a long way toward making the woman whose love language is quality time feel heard, understood, and loved.

Hugs and Kisses: The Language of Physical Touch

Until Stu and I learned about the concept of love languages, I thought I was merely a sex object to my husband, and a poor one at that! With my flat hair, flat chest, and, as I found out a few years ago, even flat eyes (I could never wear contacts), I knew I wasn't much. But, girlfriends, I was all he had! Then we learned how some individuals give and receive love primarily through physical touch. A hug in the kitchen, a quick kiss in the bathroom, and especially making love take on a much deeper meaning to the husband or wife whose love language is expressed through touch. At that moment, the light went on. No wonder Stu couldn't keep his hands off me! Every time my husband reached for me, he was saying, "I love you; please love me back" louder than words ever could.

When we discovered Stu's love language was physical touch, I quit spending so much of our hard-earned money on material things he didn't appreciate. Next, I asked him, "Do you want quality or quantity in our lovemaking?" He replied, "Quantity, every time!" I threw all my energy into speaking his love language.

Our four children were ages nine months through five years when we first heard about the five languages of love. As you can imagine, I lived in a constant state of exhaustion, so it was actually freeing for me to realize I didn't have to knock myself out in a hundred different ways to show Stu my love for him. What he wanted was me—physically. At the same time, he began putting more effort into making me feel loved in the ways I wanted, which were gifts and words. Before long, both of our love tanks were filled to overflowing instead of running on fumes and close to empty. We established a positive cycle of giving and receiving love in the ways that were most meaningful to one another. In turn, our love life was greatly enhanced on every level.

Mercy Sex

One fly in the ointment of all these new expressions of love, however, was finding out I didn't need or want physical intimacy as often as my husband. How could I continue to show Stu love by speaking his language of physical touch when often I was so tired I couldn't see straight? Dr. John Gray wrote in *Mars and Venus in the Bedroom,* "While many books talk about taking time for the woman to have a pleasurable experience, none seem to talk about the man's legitimate need to *not* take a lot of time…. To be patient and regularly take the time a woman needs in sex, a man needs to enjoy an occasional quickie."[5] How I wish I had read Dr. Gray's book in the beginning years of our marriage! It would have taken so much pressure off me *and* Stu.

Fortunately, God is the source of all truth, and He helped me to see I could give the gift of intimacy to my husband even if I wasn't in the mood. I privately called these encounters "mercy sex." Please understand I didn't let Stu know this is what I called it, but in my mind I made the decision, as the Lord has had mercy on me, so I could have mercy on my husband! The result? Stu was immensely pleased with this expression of love, and I received joy knowing I made him so happy.

Don't worry if you know you couldn't possibly keep up with your husband's sexual appetite. Instead, concentrate on taking care of him if this is his love language, and see if a new intimacy doesn't blossom between the two of you. Trust me, if he is a typical man, he will adore you!

Exceptions to the Rule

Every time I teach on the language of physical touch, at least one wife lets me know that *she* is the one who needs to feel love through the language of touch, both sexually and nonsexually. She then goes on to explain that unfortunately, for a variety of reasons, lovemaking with her husband has virtually ceased. The more she requests, the more he withdraws. If this is your predicament, my heart goes out to you, but please don't lose hope.

Dr. Janet Wolfe states in *What to Do When He Has a Headache* reasons why "men seem to be losing interest in sex."[6]

- Changing sex roles in our culture, meaning the man is no longer the pursuer
- The intimidation some men feel when confronted by the newly aggressive and supercapable woman
- A fear of closeness
- New and greater expectations placed on husbands by women who want more from their husbands emotionally and are not afraid to let them know
- Feelings of overwork and overstress
- Pressure to meet their wives' sexual needs
- Overcrowded schedules or a lack of time
- Basic boredom in the bedroom
- Marital conflict
- Sexual dysfunction
- Anxiety over unwanted pregnancy
- Various medical conditions or medications

As a Christian wife, how can you respond when your husband doesn't seem willing or able to physically connect with you? Your first line of defense, as in every situation, is to take your concerns to God in prayer. Pour out your pain before the Lord and tell Him all that is in your heart. You don't need to be embarrassed. After all, our heavenly Father is the one who created marriage in the first place. Sexual intimacy was His plan and gift for married couples to experience a oneness not found in any other relationship.

Next, after asking the Lord to prepare your husband's heart, have a talk with your man and tell him what you need and how you feel. You may even want to explain about the love languages if he has never heard this concept before. Try to let him know physical touch is one of the main avenues through which love is communicated to you. And be sure to add that you are more than willing to focus on expressing affection in ways that are meaningful to him. You might even dialogue with him to explore what those would be.

Be careful not to approach your spouse with a demanding attitude. Author Shannon Etheridge wrote about a time when she was playing with her son. Instead of saying, "Look, Mommy," he would reach up and grab her chin to get her attention. The author naturally found this irritating and would look at the toys only to get him to stop. She explained this same scenario is often played out with our husbands.[7] When we demand they meet a certain need we have, we may get what we want but not in the spirit we had hoped for. Or even worse, they may reject us altogether because they feel forced.

> When we demand they meet a certain need we have, we may get what we want but not in the spirit we had hoped for.

Finally, be patient and find joy in even the baby steps your spouse may take. If you haven't made love for a while, but he is willing to give you a backrub, be thankful! If you are making love but not nearly as often as you'd like, try to be content with the times you are intimate. If you want more nonsexual touching and your husband agrees to hold your hand while you're watching television, let him know how much this means to you. You may be in a season in which you need to lower your expectations and be content with the little expressions of love that take place between you and your husband.

Closing Thoughts

I hope you're excited to speak your husband's love language and help him understand yours. But what if you go to great lengths to show him how much you care—and you don't get an enthusiastic response from him? Or even worse, he gives you a negative or suspicious reaction to your display of affection? First, consider whether you have missed his primary love language. If you think this might be the case, don't get discouraged and give up. Try other ways of showing your spouse you care.

> Just as an unused pump needs water to prime it, the empty heart may need to hear its love language spoken more than once before it will talk back.

Next, ask yourself whether or not your spouse has gone for a long time without his love language being spoken. He may be feeling empty. If this is true, keep in mind that just as an unused pump needs water to prime it, the empty heart may need to hear its love language spoken more than once before it will talk back. The keys are persistence, patience, and enjoyment of one another even when things aren't perfect.

What if you decide, "But I want *all five* love languages spoken to me on a regular basis"? It's true that each language is a wonderful expression of love, but keeping track of how much and how often your husband demonstrates his love for you will only breed dissatisfaction within your heart. Proverbs 30:15 offers a good lesson on contentment: "The leech has two daughters. 'Give! Give!' they cry." One definition of a leech is a "person who clings to another to gain some personal advantage; a parasite."[8] When your husband looks at you, do you want him to see a sweet, loving wife or a clingy, self-centered woman? I already know which one you'll choose.

LAUGH AND PLAY

There is ... a season for every activity ... and a time to laugh.

Ecclesiastes 3:1, 4

As a little girl, how did you bond with your friends? Wasn't it through the countless hours spent laughing and playing? You ran through the sprinklers on a hot, summer day or put on dress-up clothes and pretended to be all grown up like Mom. Maybe you and your girlfriends played with dolls or did somersaults on the lawn. Then, as you grew older, your time together changed to giggling on the phone about the cute boys in your class, giving each other manicures and pedicures, and experimenting with hair and makeup. These shared experiences helped create an emotional closeness that connected you to your friends.

Secret 3

Now that you're married, it's really not that different. Did you know that for the typical husband, spending recreational time with you, his wife, ranks second only to his desire for sexual intimacy with you?[1] Look at the marketing structure of the recreation industry. They know that men spend more money on boats, sporting events, sports equipment, and gym memberships than women. Furthermore, think back to when you and your husband first dated. Play served as an important vehicle for getting to know one another. However, you don't have to be married very long to discover this aspect of an emotionally close and passionate marriage is quickly forgotten. Somewhere between piles of laundry and paying the bills, full-time jobs and keeping the lawn mowed, many couples forget to have fun.

> Just as nature has her different seasons, so does every marriage.

If this sounds depressingly familiar, please don't give up! Just as nature has her different seasons, so does every marriage. Is your favorite season spring-time, when trees are beginning to bud and thousands of blossoms fill the air with their sweet perfume? Or is it summer with its bright, blue skies and hot, lazy days? Perhaps you're energized by autumn's colorful hues and the brisk snap of cooler nights or by winter's quiet beauty of snow's peaceful stillness. If you're like me, it's hard to say which one is best because each offers a different quality to enjoy. It's the same with marriage: Each stage has its own particular beauty and challenges.

Before you resign yourself to a no-fun policy between you and your husband until (a) the kids grow up, (b) you inherit a large sum of money, or (c) all the chores are finished around the house, let's explore how you can be your husband's recreational companion through all the seasons of your life together.

Springtime—When Love Is New

"Nothing is so beautiful as spring."[2] In Colorado, where we live, we welcome the first, warm breath of spring with open arms. The signs of life beginning to stir after the long, chilling winter are abundant everywhere. Newborn colts follow their mothers cautiously about on teetering legs while, in nearby fields, stallions kick up their heels. When you first fell in love, didn't you also feel like kicking up your heels? Poets and romantics alike agree nothing compares to the giddy springtime of new love.

The springtime of a relationship includes dating, the wedding, the honeymoon, and the early years of marriage. In this season, couples do almost everything together. When you and your husband began to date, it wasn't hard to find activities you enjoyed together, was it? Most of the time just being together was enough; it didn't matter what the activity was. Many of my college girlfriends and I liked to watch our guys play their favorite team sport. Baseball, football, or basketball took on new meaning and excitement when the man you planned to marry was on the court or playing field. Women try awfully hard during the springtime of a relationship to please the man in their life. Therefore, many men marry, not realizing we don't really like football or basketball as much as they thought we did. We like our men, and that is enough.

What were some of the recreational activities you and your husband engaged in when you were dating and first married? Have you continued doing any of these on a regular basis? Playing together is vital to maintaining emotional closeness and physical desire in marriage. The old saying "The couple who prays together, stays together" has much truth in it. But so does the variation: "The couple who *plays* together stays together." Even the word *recreation* reveals why we shouldn't discount it. It means to "restore, refresh, and

> Playing together is vital to maintaining emotional closeness and physical desire in marriage.

create anew; to put fresh life into the body or mind, through play, amusement, or relaxation."[3] That's truth every relationship can benefit from.

Love Is in the Air

The springtime years of a relationship are usually the easiest season for a man and woman to find time and energy for one another. Both of you are probably able to work, so finances tend not to be an issue. Babies usually haven't arrived on the scene yet, and your parents aren't advanced enough in years to have major health problems. I know this picture is a generalization, but this is what many young people in love and newly married experience.

If real life does barge in, you have the confidence of youth and young love to look for an alternative. If you don't have much money, you know you can enjoy hiking, camping, walking, or biking together. If you do have a baby early on, you quickly learn how portable these little people really are. If your parents become ill, you have the energy and reserve to cope in ways that markedly decrease as you get older. If you're stuck with nothing to do, you are usually so much in love, it doesn't matter. Even if you are older when you meet your first love, or find love again, the excitement and those euphoric feelings are still the same.

In the springtime of life, most women are quite health and diet conscious. They watch what they eat and make time to exercise. What you may not realize is how attractive this is to the average guy. Once you understand the high value men place on recreation, you can see why they would be drawn to a woman who is active and takes care of herself. One of the biggest complaints I hear is that a husband discovers the woman he married isn't as committed to keeping in shape as he thought she was. Neither is she interested in participating in the recreational activities that drew them together in the first place. Your husband's zest for life and pursuit of athletics doesn't magically disappear after the wedding ceremony.

Motorcycle Mama

Chad and Rachel used to ride his Harley-Davidson motorcycle during the springtime of their life together. Then, along came their babies, which motivated Rachel to stop riding. Soon after, financial pressures forced Rachel back to work full-time. The motorcycle was sold, and as the years sped by, Chad and Rachel had less and less time for each other, including recreating together. Then, four years ago, Chad shocked Rachel by asking for a divorce. Rachel agreed to separate but asked Chad if he would wait to act on his desire for a divorce.

In the meantime, with the kids grown and moving out of the house, Rachel went out and bought her own Harley-Davidson. Unbeknownst to Chad, she took classes in rider instruction and outfitted herself with a helmet and safety leathers.

Chad called her up one day to talk. She said, "Why don't we meet at your apartment?" She pulled up on her motorcycle and Chad went crazy! He couldn't believe Rachel would go to such lengths to show how much she still loved him. With tears in his eyes he said, "I can't believe you remembered." Rachel replied, "How could I ever forget? Those were some of the best years of our lives."

> If romance is a key to sexual intimacy in a woman's heart, then recreational companionship is a key for men.

On the one hand, you might think Chad's reaction was superficial, but as a woman you need to understand, if romance is a key to sexual intimacy in a woman's heart, then recreational companionship is a key for men.

What does your husband like to do? Of those activities he enjoys, which could you participate in? Can you remember activities you used to share with him? Being your husband's recreational companion isn't necessarily limited to sports. Maybe you married a computer guy who loves board games and art museums. Find at least one or two of your husband's interests and passions that you could do with him.

Finding the Balance

Most men have at least one pastime their wives either can't do with them or wouldn't want to. My husband plays basketball at 5:30 in the morning with a bunch of other guys. I don't want to be in a cold, dark gym in the middle of the night (which is what 5:30 a.m. is to me), and he doesn't want or need me there. Other men I know like to play cards with "the boys" one night a week or to push themselves to their physical limit by mountain biking up trails most of their wives wouldn't even want to hike on!

There are two theories on couples spending leisure time engaged in activities together. On one end of the spectrum we find those experts who advocate having a little separateness. He likes to golf; she likes to go to scrapbooking parties. He likes to play extreme sports; she keeps up with her dance lessons. Two women at one of my speaking engagements said their husbands were avid ATVers. They packed up the kids, took along books and walking shoes, and caught up on some much-needed girl time while cheering their men on as they tore around the tracks and got filthy.

My relationship with my husband has stayed close even though we have separate interests. I have always loved to horseback ride. In the meantime, Stu stays involved in his basketball and softball leagues. But we always try to carve out time for walks or hikes through the woods during the week and a date on the weekend.

On the other end of the spectrum are those who advocate that you should "only engage in those recreational activities that both you and your spouse can enjoy together."[4] Marriage and family counselor Dr. Willard Harley wrote that when he first married, he was president of his university's chess club and often enjoyed the game with his wife. After a few months of marriage, however, she informed him she wasn't interested in playing chess—or any other game with him for that matter—since he always won. Because of the time commitment chess involves, he quit playing and together they found pastimes they could both enjoy.

He also recommends that husbands and wives spend at least fifteen uninterrupted hours a week together, some of which are spent on a shared recreational activity. If a husband and wife could both commit to this counselor's advice, they'd probably have a fantastic marriage. How could they not? All that time spent laughing and playing together would form an incredibly strong bond of love.

If you share Dr. Harley's plan with your husband and he goes for it, you can skip the rest of this chapter, because your marriage will already sizzle in this area! For the rest of us, however, I would suggest experimenting with spending larger and larger amounts of time together on what you both enjoy. See how much togetherness your relationship can bear. Find your threshold of compatibility—that point at which you don't have time for the activities you used to enjoy alone or you begin bickering. At that point, take a step back from so much togetherness, so that instead of feeling pressured, you are both left wanting more.

In springtime, more than any other season, both relationally and in nature, we sense "love is in the air." But, as we are all too aware, springtime doesn't last forever.

Summer—When Love Bears Fruit

Summer is the time of year when much of what you hoped for has come true. The flowers you planted in spring are now in full bloom. Days are longer and nights are shorter, so you have more time for playing, swimming, camping, and exploring. Maybe you've moved into your own home, and your children fill the sunny days with their smiles. And if you're really fortunate, you're lulled to sleep on summer nights by the sound of crickets chirping in unison to your children's quiet breathing. This season does hold special delights, but it can also bring stifling heat and nasty mosquito bites, the "dog days of summer."

Summertime in a marriage relationship may be as wonderful as the idyllic season I described, but it can also be a time of rude awakenings … literally! Not only if you have newborn babies, but in all sorts of other ways that aren't limited to having children at all. The high expectations and idealism that characterized love's springtime can dry up and leave you feeling like you're in the desert. Often, the end of the storybook life we envisioned occurs most frequently when we've been married from seven to ten years. This phenomenon is so common it is known as the "seven-year itch," a vulnerable time in a marriage. Some spouses are tempted to escape the pressures and responsibilities and start over with someone new, thinking they can stay forever in the springtime season of a relationship.

For our purposes, the summer of your love relationship begins around the seventh year of marriage or when you have children, whichever comes first, and lasts until your children begin leaving home. By this time, the first stimulating flush of new love has worn off, which isn't necessarily a bad thing. Our minds and bodies weren't designed to sustain that degree of excitement over the long haul. We would wear out! Summertime love is when all the hopes we've had from the beginning of a relationship finally bear fruit. Along with the joy of seeing those dreams come true, however, is the reality of the tremendous responsibilities required to maintain those dreams. A home of your own means a mortgage. Cars need to be paid for and maintained. Yards must be taken care of. Even the blessing of a newborn baby comes with the realization that you are now on call, twenty-four hours a day, seven days a week.

Surviving a Drought

During the summertime of our marriage, I felt like we were in the middle of one long, unending drought. As I mentioned in chapter 1, both of our mothers and grandmothers, whom we were very close to, became ill and died in the five years I gave birth to our four children. Because of these sad circumstances, we spent far too many hours in hospitals and at funerals. We said goodbye to the first little home we'd bought in California and moved into a three-bedroom duplex when I was pregnant with our fourth child so we could afford to live on the meager income from our brand-new business. We lost thousands of dollars when the business failed, and the value of another home we bought at the peak of the real estate market tanked when it was time for us to sell. I also experienced

> Even in the best and easiest of marriages, words such as *fatigue, exhaustion, stretched thin, work pressures, busyness,* and *budgets* come quickly to mind during this season.

severe health issues during that time, and when our children were three to eight years old, I was hospitalized for twelve days due to a life-threatening reaction to an antibiotic. Add to this the normal ups and downs of being married, plus the waning excitement of new love, and we had a prescription for disaster.

Has the first blush of your new love worn off? Perhaps you are one of the fortunate few who has been spared many of the hardships a drought could bring to your relationship. If so, I rejoice in the Lord with you! But even in the best and easiest of marriages, words such as *fatigue, exhaustion, stretched thin, work pressures, busyness,* and *budgets* come quickly to mind during this season.

When you're overwhelmed by mountains of laundry and the legitimate demands of children, how can you find the time, energy, or desire to be your husband's recreational companion? It's tough. But even in the midst of jobs, church work, parenting four preteens to teens, and major health concerns, my husband wouldn't let me get away with bailing on him, and I have been forever grateful.

Forced Blessings

A few summers ago I was doing my annual good deed of volunteering for a week at a local Christian camp. I called home one night to check in with Stu to see how he was doing without all of the usual chaos, since three of our four children were at camp with me. He was talking very fast over the phone, which is unusual for this southern giant of a man who normally speaks slow as molasses. I soon found out why: He'd just bought two jet skis and a trailer to pull them! How fun, you might say, but he did this all without even asking me. I quickly and heatedly reminded him of this fact, to which he replied, "But you knew!"

I asked, "How was I supposed to know?"

"Remember when we were on the lake last summer and I told you that I wanted to get some of these babies for us?" he replied.

That was it. One sentence in June translated into thousands

of dollars spent on jet skis for our family. The worst part of the whole affair was that we had to attend a wedding the next afternoon of a sweet, young couple from our church. At one point in the ceremony they did a foot washing for each other, promising to love and serve one another as Christ loved and served the church. It was all I could do to not stand up and shout to the bride, "You don't know what you're doing!! You don't know what you're getting yourself into! He could go out and buy jet skis and not even ask you and you can't divorce him for this!" (I checked the Bible thoroughly. There are absolutely no Scriptures permitting us to divorce our husbands if they buy big toys without our permission.)

Much to my chagrin, for all my whining and complaining and moaning, the jet skis have turned out to be a great way for us to bond recreationally. And not just for Stu and me—our entire family has grown closer. During our dating days, we used to ride his motorcycle, but I gave that up long ago. I found when I got on the back of our jet skis and wrapped my arms around Stu's middle-aged tummy, feelings of love and tenderness and fond memories surfaced as we flew over the water. This was in addition to all the fun and excitement of the new memories we were creating. (An added bonus is that the jet skis brought our teens and their friends camping with us often over the years, when they may otherwise have stayed home.)

Mini Moments

Are you currently in the summer of your marriage? Does it feel like ages since you and your husband have had fun? Another way to bring laughter and a spirit of playfulness to your marriage is to turn "mini moments" into something special. Stu and I like to share funny bumper stickers we've seen. My all-time favorite says, "Of all the things I've lost, I miss my mind the most!" And my husband's is, "I may be getting older, but I refuse to grow up!" (Those of you who know us are chuckling—there's a little truth in most humor!) We also collect jokes we've read or heard and bring them out when we want to liven things up.

One of the biggest issues couples face in the summertime of marriage is who will watch the kids while Mom and Dad are connecting. This is one area where you have to be determined to find a solution, or your life as a couple will slip by during this busy season. The couple willing to look hard to find solutions will find many options. Reliable teens are always a good choice. If money is a concern, look into a babysitting co-op. Of course the best alternative, if it is available to you, is letting Grandma and Grandpa have your little ones for an hour or two.

Forget the Floor

Another obstacle that prohibits couples from spending time together during the summer of their lives is feeling that chores and responsibilities simply must be taken care of right then. How can I justify playing golf with my husband when the carpet needs to be vacuumed and Jamie's room looks like a tornado hit it? Some personalities can live with their homes being less than perfect. If you happen to be one of these, you probably can't relate to what I just wrote! Some of us perfectionists, however, really struggle with having fun when duty calls. A strong work ethic is not a bad trait, but we need to relax—and let him relax!—now and then so that we can nurture

> A strong work ethic is not a bad trait, but we need to relax—and let him relax!—now and then so that we can nurture our relationships with our husbands.

our relationships with our husbands. (Admit it! You've got a "honey-do" list a mile long!)

Find a sitter, let some of the housework go, and make time this week to talk with your husband about picking a recreational activity you can do together. It can be either an activity the two of you enjoyed during the springtime of your relationship or a new one you'd both like to try. If your energy is low from the demands of housework and small children, see if your sweetie would be willing to take you out for dinner or on a picnic. Then, the next time you plan an outing, let him pick the activity. If it's one you aren't too excited about, go along with his suggestion; you might just like it.

Mike decided he and Brenda should try bowling together. He knew she wasn't in top shape physically, but he was a big sports buff and wanted to do something together that required physical exertion. Brenda went that first night to the bowling alley with some misgivings. Bowling seemed kind of "low class" to her, and besides, what if she threw gutter balls? Much to her surprise, she didn't perform badly and found she actually liked it. Mike, in turn, was so pleased she'd made the effort that he happily alternated their date night of bowling with taking Brenda to dinner and a movie. As their kids got older, they started taking the entire family.

Who would have ever thought a bowling alley could be so romantic? This couple that played together *did* stay together, and everyone in the family reaped the benefits.

Autumn—When Love Embraces Change

Traditionally, fall is a season bursting with activity. School begins, and our celebrations revolve around a time when farmers brought in the rich harvest that would see them through winter. The leaves on the trees are an artist's palette of reds, oranges, browns, and yellows, and we light the first fires in the hearth to ward off the evening chill. Even though many autumn days are still warm and sunny, the nights remind us that winter is coming.

Autumn as a marriage season is so full of transition, it refuses to slip by unnoticed. After decades of sameness, everything seems to change. Your once predictable body begins shutting down its menstrual cycle, and a whole range of emotional and physical issues makes you feel as if you're on one, long roller-coaster ride. Unfortunately, instead of being fun, this ride makes you queasy, and all you want to do is get off.

Perhaps you had a houseful of kids and stayed at home or only worked part-time. You spent your time trying to catch your breath in the midst of a hectic schedule, and the calendar over-flowed with activities. Suddenly, one morning the house is silent, and you wander around with time on your hands, some-thing you couldn't imagine just a few short years ago. Even more disturbing, you sit at the dinner table—just you and your husband—and realize you hardly know this man across from you. Like Halloween night, the season of autumn in a marriage can be downright scary!

It is at this critical juncture in a marriage that some men and women cut their losses and try to replace the incredible loneliness they feel with a new relationship. If a marriage has always been difficult, one or both of the partners may decide it isn't worth the effort anymore. If it has been a relatively easy, low-maintenance marriage, one of you may be bored with the other.

The autumn season usually occurs in our forties and fifties. A man in his forties may be confronted with the reality he is never going to achieve what he imagined in his career. The financial goals he set may not have materialized, and he's old enough to realize that they probably never will. On the other hand, if he has been wildly successful and has attained everything his heart has desired, he may find life—and his wife—dull as dishwater.

Add to this the physical changes his body undergoes. He can't run down the court as fast as he used to or throw a baseball as far. Or worse, the sports he once enjoyed can now actually land him in the hospital. And even more critical for him, his sexual desire and responses may have begun to slow. If he is a typical male and this is happening, mark my words, he is sure he's as good as dead!

Turn the Ship Around

Now, before you get too discouraged and don't want to read any further, know that I believe in getting the bad news out of the way so we can concentrate on the good stuff. Picture your marriage as a long voyage on a ship. Autumn is the perfect season to turn the ship around and bring her to a safe harbor for winter and the end of the journey.

You and your husband will start having more alone time during the autumn years. Therefore, take this time to address any issues in your marriage that may have prevented oneness over the years, prayerfully seeking the Lord as to how best to resolve them. If you or your husband like to read, find a book on the topic you think would be helpful and start there.

If your husband doesn't like to read, here is a method that works well with many men. Let your sweetie know of a book you'd love for him to read because you think it will help your marriage be the best it can be. In return, ask him to tell you one thing he would like you to do for him that will show you are serious about taking care of his needs as well. For example, Debbie really wanted her husband to read the book *His Needs, Her Needs* with her, at least the section on her needs. Since her hubby wasn't much of a reader, she asked Matt, "Is there anything you'd like me to do for you, since I'd like you to read this book with me?" He responded with a wink and a grin and said, "You know what I'd always like more of." (Read between the lines, girlfriends.) Debbie smiled back and said, "You're on. I'm glad to do whatever it takes to motivate you!"

I know this sounds simplistic, but you wouldn't believe the number of women who are genuinely disappointed when I tell them it isn't fair to ask their husbands to do something particularly meaningful for them if they, the wives, are unwilling to do what would be meaningful for their spouses.

> Autumn is definitely the season to redefine what recreational activity means to you and your husband.

If books, prayer, and talking with each other aren't helping, please find a good Christian counselor to begin moving in the right direction. You've probably invested at least twenty years in one another by the time you reach autumn. It would be a tragedy to let your relationship wither and die after all those years together. Or, if you've lived in an unspoken truce while the kids were home, now is the time to put down the white flag and move toward intimacy and emotional oneness.

Redefine "Fun"

In the autumn season of marriage, recreational activities you have always enjoyed with your husband can be enjoyed more fully. Walking, hiking, biking, swimming, golf, and—here's a fun one—dancing are all pastimes you can still share with your spouse that don't require the same level of stamina and fitness you had in your twenties. One super-jock husband we know

now plays cribbage and dominoes, something he never had the patience for when he was younger. His wife likes this change in their marriage because she actually wins once in a while! Although Bob is still highly competitive, he and Janey are on equal footing now that they play more board and card games.

Sandy is married to Ron, a gentle, quiet man. Sandy, however, is highly verbal, and Ron's silence drives her crazy at times, especially when he wants to take her to a ball game. To help pass the time, she purchased a scorecard and filled in the lineup, which made the game fly by. It helped her pay attention and even got Ron talking more because he'd lean over and ask her the latest stats. Way to go, Sandy!

Valerie is married to an avid fisherman who is so good that a television producer noticed him at a fishing tournament and asked if he'd like to host a fishing show. Valerie now flies all over the country to be with her husband while he fishes. If it's just the two of them and he's out for recreation, she brings a folding chair and the latest book she's reading. If he's hosting a show, she stands back by the cinematographers, brings everyone soft drinks, and cheers her man on.

Autumn is definitely the season to redefine what recreational activity means to you and your husband. For instance, perhaps your husband is a whiz in the kitchen. When you don't have to worry about the

> If the purpose of recreating together is to create fond memories and build closeness, I know of no better way to do so than to participate in a ministry with your husband.

time constraints of picking up children and babysitters, a monthly dinner club with a group of friends can make for a great night of entertainment. Even if your husband doesn't like to cook, I've never met a man who doesn't like to eat.

Ministry Companions

On a different note, have you ever considered ministry to others as a form of recreation? If the purpose of recreating together is to create fond memories and build closeness, I know of no better way to do so than to participate in a ministry with your husband. When Stu and I were in college, we had a wonderful, godly youth pastor named Scott Farmer. Scott encouraged his flock not just to marry someone we had fun with but to marry someone with whom we could partner to further the kingdom of God.

In the autumn of our lives, we usually have the time, resources, and wisdom to pour ourselves into ministry with more impact than when we were young. However, what often happens by this stage is husbands and wives go their separate ministry ways. She teaches Bible study to women on Tuesdays, while he works Saturdays fixing up homes for

> You'll find the memories you make serving God as a couple—especially when people are touched and lives are changed—bring a new level of emotional closeness and spiritual oneness between the two of you.

lower income families with others in the church. I'm not advocating abandoning your individual ministries, but I would encourage couples to consider finding a way to serve together, too.

Furthermore, as we get older and heaven becomes more of a reality, the verses in the Bible about storing up treasure in heaven (see Matt. 6:20) take on greater meaning. Are we focusing only on our time on earth, or are we also consciously making deposits in heaven? Ministry with your husband could be a short-term mission trip. It will change your perspective forever and for the better. Closer to home, the two of you could lead a young-marrieds class, work with the youth in your church, counsel hurting couples, or invite tired church staff over for an evening of dinner, fellowship, and refreshment.

Anyone who has ever been involved with true ministry knows it isn't just more hard work. Joy, laughter, and a profound sense of peace intermingle with the prayers and tears. You'll find the memories you make serving God as a couple—especially when people are touched and lives are changed—bring a new level of emotional closeness and spiritual oneness between the two of you.

Winter—When Love Endures

Winter in a marriage is like winter in different regions of the world: It may be harsh or pleasant, depending on where you live. Regardless, beauty can always be found. Everyone knows that it is in the midst of ice and snow, freezing winds and long, dark nights that you enjoy skiing and sledding, ice skating and hot chocolate. Kids build crooked snowmen, families share cozy nights, and, best of all, we get to celebrate Christmas.

Many couples enjoy the winter season of marriage thanks to better nutrition and medical breakthroughs, which have led to longer lives and better health. We know many older couples who explore a new country every year, go on six-month mission trips, swim, play basketball, and take part in the new senior pastime that includes exercise as well as friendship: mall walking!

Quieter pursuits also bring pleasure and bond couples to one another: Reading aloud is a great way to discover a story, share insights, and keep your mind sharp. It's like watching movies together—only better—for some couples.

Winter, more than any other season in a marriage, is the time when the foundation of your marriage—your faith, your shared history, your vows, and your enduring love—steadies you through the worst of life's storms. Most of us will experience the season of winter in our marriage when we're senior citizens. As our strength fades and our minds falter, we pray we'll have the energy and health to enjoy the golden years with our beloved.

But sadly, winter can come to a marriage not only when our lives wind down. What if an illness or accident shatters your dreams of recreating together or becoming globe-trotters? Like an early frost in autumn, winter rudely interrupts and comes before its time. When it does, can you still find opportunities to laugh and play?

A True Fairy Tale

Dear friends of ours felt the sharp sting of winter only one short year after they married. Lance and Deidre met in high school. Their teasing flirtation quickly developed into the strong, caring relationship they still enjoy today. Young and in love, Lance and Deidre spent every moment together. Like many young people their age in the mountain community where they lived, they hiked forest trails and played on co-ed softball teams. They skied the Rocky Mountains' white slopes in winter and played in the cold, clear lakes in summer. Deidre was so in love with Lance that she passed up an opportunity to study art on scholarship in Italy. And Lance made sure she never regretted that decision; he asked Deidre to marry him. Right out of high school, Deidre walked down the aisle with Lance, who was twenty-one, and began their new life together. It was the springtime of their love, and they had everything to look forward to.

For a year, their lives continued on much the same as before. Then one day Deidre felt a lump in her abdomen. With the optimism of youth, she wasn't too concerned but still saw a doctor. After a few tests, she learned it was a benign tumor embedded in a major artery and would have to be removed. Lance and Deidre, their friends and family, prayed all would go well the morning of surgery, and she went under anesthesia reasonably assured it would.

The surgery took less time than expected, and hopes flew high when Deidre was wheeled into recovery. Groggy from the anesthesia, she gave Lance a small smile, relieved that the worst was over. Then the nightmare began. The surgeon had failed to properly tie off the major artery, and Deidre hemorrhaged. Alarms rang, and the hospital urgently paged additional doctors back to the operating room. Lance sat in disbelief and prayed God would save his young wife.

The Lord heard Lance's prayer, and Deidre's life was spared. But with that answered prayer came a host of other difficulties. Deidre was left with multiple handicaps stemming from blood loss and lack of oxygen to her brain. Deidre went into the operating room a vibrant nineteen-year-old with all the promises of youth and health. She emerged a shell of the woman she had been. Unable to walk or talk, she was barely able to communicate that she understood those around her. Lance wiped the tears that rolled down her cheeks because she was unable to do so.

Deidre's family was stunned. In their pain and grief, her parents made what they thought was a reasonable offer to Lance. Deidre's mother said, "Lance, you're young. You have your whole life ahead of you. We're Deidre's family; we love her. We'll bring her home and take care of her, and you can go on with your life."

Only twenty-two at the time, Lance saw his marriage to Deidre plunge into winter with no warning or preparation. He looked Deidre's mother in the eye and quietly but firmly said, "No. I made a vow to Deidre before God and all of our friends and family. I'm going to stay with her and take care of her."

Four months later, Deidre was released from the hospital. Three years later, when their little girl was born, Lance bathed baby Courtney and taught Deidre how to change her diaper. Since Deidre couldn't do many ordinary tasks, let alone recreational activities, one of their pastimes became Deidre's physical therapy with Lance while they watched the latest sports event on television.

Fast forward to twenty-five years later, when Stu and I met Lance and Deidre. It took only a few moments of time with this wonderful couple to pick up on Deidre's now slight disabilities and Lance's protective concern. Deidre still needs him to tie her shoes and help in other small ways. But she is able to do all the accounting for a successful business, drives her own car, and is responsible for a weekly Bible study in a women's prison several miles away.

Deidre can't do many of the activities she and Lance once shared, but she is one of the best recreational companions to a husband I have ever met. When Lance wants to hunt pheasant in Kansas, Deidre brings a book and goes along for the drive. When he goes fishing at the local reservoir, Deidre is right there in the boat beside him. Last summer, Deidre trained several days a week and hiked one of Colorado's fourteen-thousand-foot peaks with Lance and some friends. Deidre is my role model for the kind of recreational companion I would like to be to Stu, and, as you can guess, it is just one of the many reasons Lance is devoted to her.

As I speak to various groups, I've yet to meet a wife with the same challenges my dear friend Deidre has faced. No matter what obstacles you think stand in your way—small children, finances, lack of time, work schedules, household responsibilities, or health issues—few of us have a good excuse not to be the best recreational companion to our husbands we can be. Remember, a little fun goes a long way toward brightening your outlook on life and keeping your husband madly in love with you all the seasons of your marriage.

LIFE'S LITTLE LUXURIES

Every good and perfect gift is from above, coming down from the Father.

James 1:17

When you hear the word *luxury*, what do you think of? Most of us imagine a dream cruise aboard a chartered yacht or a second honeymoon on a private, tropical island somewhere in the South Seas. We think of mink coats, four-carat diamond rings, and servants to wait on us hand and foot, available at our every beck and call.

But let's talk about delightful diversions that are accessible to almost everyone, no matter what your economic situation. If you don't give yourself permission to partake in these little luxuries of life, your marriage will probably have more fizzle than sizzle! For our purposes, we're going to use one of the definitions of the term *luxury* from *Webster's:* "anything contributing to enjoyment usually considered unnecessary to life and health."[1] When described that way, we're allowed to include a lot, aren't we?

Secret 4

If you have tried to follow and apply the secrets for sizzle we've discussed so far, hopefully you've lowered your expectations of perfection. You have discovered your husband's love language, and he yours, and are trying to speak them on a regular basis.

You're also spending more leisure time together again by reconnecting through recreation so an atmosphere of fun continues in your marriage.

Once you and your husband are laughing and playing more, letting go of perfection, and communicating your love in meaningful ways, a natural outcome should be an increase in your desire for one another. Then we can apply secret number four to make your marriage sizzle: Learn to take advantage of life's little luxuries. You may think you're being selfish at first, but these treats enhance the quality of your relationship so much, you'll soon wonder why you tried to live without them!

The Luxury of Privacy

For years I debated including the notion of privacy as a secret for emotional closeness and passion in a marriage, because it seemed so obvious. Of course a husband and wife need privacy to maintain intimacy in their relationship. And I'm not just referring to physical intimacy. The private moments you share with your husband, emotionally and physically, are what set your relationship apart from any other relationship on the face of the earth. You can let go of perfection with your family, you can speak a friend's love language, and you can certainly enjoy recreation with lots of people other

> The private moments you share with your husband, emotionally and physically, are what set your relationship apart from any other relationship on the face of the earth.

than your spouse. But the areas of your marriage that are surrounded by the hedge of privacy are where your marriage should diverge and look different from any other relationship you have.

In our current culture, it's considered appropriate to expose almost every facet of life for public consumption. Sleeping, eating, and even bodily functions normally reserved for the bathroom are all fair game. That's why TV reality shows are so successful. I don't know about you, but I for one don't believe in treating all aspects of life equally. They're not. Some parts of life, including our innermost thoughts and desires and the sexual relationship, are meant to be shared with only one person—our spouse.

> One of the quiet joys of married life is the private jokes between you and your husband—the secret innuendoes that wouldn't mean a thing to anyone else but, because of your history together, can send both of you into fits of laughter.

Emotional Privacy

One of the quiet joys of married life is the private jokes between you and your husband—the secret innuendoes that wouldn't mean a thing to anyone else but, because of your history together, can send both of you into fits of laughter. One word from Stu (no, I'm not going to tell you which word!), and I know exactly what he means, what he's thinking, and even the thought process that brought him to that point. Emotional privacy is the closeness that develops between a couple through the years, so just a look,

> **Emotional privacy is the closeness that develops between a couple through the years, so just a look, a glance, a touch, a smirk, or a word speaks volumes.**

a glance, a touch, a smirk, or a word speaks volumes.

On a more serious level, one trait that characterizes a close marriage is the understanding that certain information is off-limits to anyone other than our spouse. During our private times together, we want to be free to talk about intensely personal issues: our hopes and fears, wishes and dreams, deep hurts and miserable failures. These confidences we share with our husbands, and no one else knows. Ideally, they reciprocate. One unmarried woman calls this gift a priceless luxury. She thinks many married women take for granted the fact that with our husbands we have a built-in sounding board for the inner life we rarely expose.

Here is one description of this type of intimacy: "These couples have been talking ... for thirty years or more.... They can talk to each other in ways they cannot talk to anyone else. He can tell her of something good he has done without fearing she will think he is bragging. He can count on her interest and understanding."[2] Wouldn't you like to be that kind of wife to your husband? I know I would.

Having a level of trust that allows sharing our innermost secrets builds emotional intimacy and closeness in a marriage like nothing else. Emotional privacy is the luxury that doesn't cost a dime; it only requires us to pay the high price of discretion and self-control.

Between us girls, we have to admit that we're usually the ones who talk indiscriminately. I know some men fall into this category, but there's got to be a reason the Bible repeatedly admonishes women to control our tongues. Proverbs 11:22 paints an unattractive picture of an overly talkative woman: "Like a gold ring in a pig's snout is a beautiful woman who shows no discretion." Likewise, when we as wives fail to be discreet, which means to "keep silent or preserve confidences when necessary,"[3] we're as useless to our husbands, and anyone else for that matter, as a fourteen-carat gold ring in the nose of a hog headed for the breakfast table.

> Emotional privacy is the luxury that doesn't cost a dime; it only requires us to pay the high price of discretion and self-control.

Treasure Trust

Has your husband ever told you something in confidence, but you were sure he wouldn't mind your bringing it up to your ladies' group for prayer? I confess I have. Because of my personality, I am much more open about personal issues than Stu is. Your husband may have several topics he wants kept between the two of you. Some likely candidates are business troubles, financial matters, his family of origin, problems that have led to counseling, and his health concerns. If you and/or your husband are currently in counseling or are experiencing a rough time in your marriage, *do not* share details with anyone who may take up an offense against your husband. Because of the dynamics of counseling, your counselor will probably advise you to have a small network of mature, godly friends you can both talk to. If you want your husband to feel secure about continuing counseling, however, what takes place in your sessions should, for the most part, stay there. Again, use discretion in deciding what you need to discuss with a trusted friend and what to withhold. The bottom line? Always ask your husband if he minds your divulging information pertaining to the two of you before you do.

Because of my speaking engagements, especially on the topic of marriage, Stu has been extremely gracious about my sharing personal information with complete strangers. I try to make sure, however, that he won't die a thousand deaths over whatever I say about him. Early in our marriage, when I started teaching Bible studies, God often corrected me through godly women. More than once our phone would ring, and a spiritually older woman would be on the other end, gently admonishing me in love about a slip of the tongue I'd made.

> Always ask your husband if he minds your divulging information pertaining to the two of you before you do.

One of the best ways I know to combat overflow of the mouth and avoid sabotaging your relationship with your husband is to pray Psalm 141:3 (NASB): "Set a guard, O LORD, over my mouth; Keep watch over the door of my lips." Thankfully, what we are unable to do on our own—especially us talkaholics—the Holy Spirit can do in and through us if we ask Him.

In some marriages, this special trust regarding what's been said in private has been violated. Either what we've shared has been repeated or, even more devastating, brought out in an argument and used as a weapon against us. If this is your situation, I pray that you will do all within your power to resolve it at once. If you betrayed your husband's trust, go to him as soon as possible. Tell him sincerely you're sorry and ask his forgiveness. If you have been a talker and have let him down in this area before, ask your husband to pray for you. Tell him you have been convicted that you have undermined the trust in your relationship, and you are willing to do whatever is necessary to restore his faith in you.

If he has been the one who has talked indiscriminately, forgive him before the Lord, and during your conversations, patiently point out which topics are for "his ears only."

One couple we know included a well-meaning but gregarious husband. In various social gatherings, he would let private information slip out—usually about other people—that should *not* have been repeated. At one point, several friends asked the wife *not* to tell her husband what they were about to say. Talk about embarrassing! Thankfully, her husband got the message. But in the meantime, his wife used tremendous discretion in her dialogues with him, withholding anything she thought could create an awkward situation if it happened to leak out.

If you are intentional about honoring the notion of emotional privacy between you and your husband, your feelings of love, closeness, and passion for one another will only deepen as the years unfold.

Too Much Togetherness

But can a marriage have too much closeness? My husband and I know several couples who work together. After painting houses or running a family business all day, they go home to even more of each other. Remarkably, these husbands and wives are extremely compatible. They never seem to tire of their spouses' company.

For some couples, however, too much time together can feel stifling and snuff out the sizzle in their relationship. Instead of trying to carve out time alone with their husbands, these women would love an hour to themselves. Since more and more people are working from home, couples may find themselves around each other 24/7. If this is a new situation, either party may feel a loss of privacy or alone time.

> If your husband is around all day and you feel yourself getting irritated, take a break by going for a walk, riding a bike, seeing a girlfriend— the possibilities are endless.

Can you keep the sizzle alive when you're with your husband all the time? The answer is yes, and to help you, here are some little luxuries you and your husband may want to indulge in.

Get Out of the House

If your husband is around all day and you feel yourself getting irritated, take a break by going for a walk, riding a bike, seeing a girlfriend—the possibilities are endless. Even if you have little ones, you can go out for the morning and get them home in time for naps. I know it may be a lot of work to pack up your babies and go, but you'll come home so refreshed, it will be worth it. Even better, ask your hubby to watch the children so you can have an hour or two of "me" time.

When our children were small and money was practically nonexistent, one of life's little luxuries for me was going to the library alone. Because I love to read, I always liked having several books around, but found I couldn't take the time to browse when the babies came with me. So every couple of weeks, I would take a Saturday morning and hang out at the library. That may not sound like the height of luxury for some of you, but it was remarkably therapeutic for me. I came home calm and with an armload of books to see me through the days ahead.

Get Him out of the House

If you're ready for some undisturbed time at home, reverse the situation I described above and ask your husband to take the kids for an outing. Many women consider time at home by themselves a luxury. Then, when you do get your alone time, do only what will recharge your battery and leave you feeling emotionally and physically energized. Some women want to soak in a hot bubble bath, surrounded by scented candles and soothing music. Our task-oriented friends may tackle an unorganized closet or garage because they love bringing order without interruptions. As Alexandra Stoddard reminds us, "Beauty plus order equals energy."[4]

Time spent home alone is also a great time to get creative. If you paint, play a musical instrument, like to decorate, or work on photo albums, this time will feel like the height of luxury to you. Spending undisturbed time with the Lord—worshipping Him, praising Him aloud, reading His Word, or writing in a prayer journal to the Lover of your soul—is the absolute best restorative ever.

Or, ask your husband nicely if he'd get some groceries, pick up a few things at the drugstore, or go to the nearest electronics store to replace that broken phone. You might also suggest he meet a friend for lunch, go to the men's weekly prayer breakfast, or work out at the local gym, if that's something he enjoys.

Work Around the House

What if your togetherness is because your husband is out of work? Gently suggest to him meaningful jobs that can be done at home. Because of the unique tensions and pressures that can arise when a man is out of work, your feelings of esteem toward your husband will increase if he's accomplishing something for the family. Plus, he'll feel better about himself.

One way to keep the sizzle going if your sweetie isn't too motivated about sprucing up the house is to reward him for a job well done—or even for just getting started if it's a big project. Wives frequently tell me they can't get their husbands to do anything around the house. My response? Pay him well in a currency he'll appreciate. That's why it's important to know your husband's love language.

After teaching this little tip at a church class, I was walking through the halls the following Sunday when a middle-aged man came up to me. Without introducing himself he shook my hand and, with a huge grin on his face, said, "I cleaned the garage this weekend." I shook his hand back, and for the life of me couldn't figure out why he would be telling me such a thing. Again, still shaking my hand, he said even more emphatically, "I cleaned the garage this weekend," and this time he added, "Twice!"

> Many everyday luxuries in life, available to every married couple, can be used to bless each other if we'll just open our eyes and take advantage of them.

His wife must have seen the puzzled look on my face, because she came to my rescue and said, "Remember what you taught us in class last week about rewarding our husbands for a chore they didn't want to do? Well, I told Paul I'd reward him if he'd clean the garage, and he did—twice!"

Don't underestimate the power of rewarding behaviors you'd like to see more of in your relationship. As human beings we respond much more readily to the positive and pleasurable than the harsh and negative. Many everyday luxuries in life, available to every married couple, can be used to bless each other if we'll just open our eyes and take advantage of them.

Barely There

For every reason you may find yourself with your husband too much, there are just as many circumstances that lead to never getting enough time together to cultivate the privacy and intimacy you crave. Once again, stage of life is a big factor. If you're in the baby years and your husband is working extra hours so you can stay home, you may wonder when you'll ever get to finish a conversation. Or maybe both of you are working full time and are traveling often. If this is your predicament, time together floats far away like a distant dream.

If small children and interruptions are constant, your marriage is like Colorado's weather: constantly shifting and unpredictable. Even with the best of intentions, you can't plan for private moments because babies and their needs are impossible to schedule. If the baby is dozing in his swing and your toddlers are mesmerized by *Sesame Street*, take your husband's hand and sit down for fifteen minutes of catch-up time. One of the keys to emotional intimacy in any relationship, but especially marriage, is frequent contact and keeping current with each other. If you do this four to five times a week, when you have a date night (notice I said *when* not *if!*), a sense of connectedness with one another will already be established.

The same principles apply if you're both working around the clock. You'll want to find short, simple ways to preserve emotional closeness with your hubby. You can e-mail a problem you'd like his perspective on, fax him an idea for a date, or (our personal favorite) pick up the phone.

Because Stu spends several hours each day visiting different customers, he spends lots of time on the road. Many years ago we learned the cell phone was a great way for us to keep in touch. Sometimes we'll talk several times a day, depending on our schedules. We've even learned to use the phone as an appropriate medium for discussing potentially volatile issues. If one of our kids has acted up, I call Stu early in the day to let him know what's happening so he can pray and process what I've shared with him throughout the day. This always works much better than springing it on him when he's tired and walks through the door.

Again, be the expert on your husband. You know his personality, and he knows yours, so keep experimenting until you discover what keeps the two of you talking and connected throughout your days.

Traveling can be especially tough on a marriage unless you've come up with constructive ways to cope. I have interviewed women whose husbands are gone at least fifty percent of the time or more. Each woman has maintained a strong, loving marriage in spite of an oftentimes absent husband. One wife loved when her husband traveled because she was such a high-energy, supermotivated woman. She would devote hours to her writing ministry, pour herself into projects around the house, and still be there for her two daughters.

Another woman struggled desperately when her husband took a job in another state and was home only on weekends. One of the biggest difficulties she faced was being independent when Greg was gone and then reverting to a more dependent role when he returned home. Other problems included discipline issues with the kids and reconnecting with Greg. During the week, Linda called the shots and made decisions for herself and the kids. Then Greg would come home and want things done differently. Add to this her thoughts and feelings that would've been discussed during the week if Greg had been home. She said it was one of the most stressful times in their marriage.

So, how can a marriage stay close and sizzle even when your spouse isn't around? Gail's husband has traveled for business most of their married life. She offers these tips for keeping the home fires burning:

- *Hold a powwow.* Before your husband leaves, discuss any issues you want addressed with the children. Then, as a family, let him tell what's expected while he's away.
- *Talk every day.* Rick calls Gail every night he's away. This helps her to empathize with any unique pressures he may experience and gives her an outlet as well. Most men aren't good at marathon talks; they do better with short sessions. A daily chat acknowledges this difference and keeps you connected. Talking every day also helps your husband combat the temptation to turn to pornography, which is too readily available in most hotel rooms. If your husband

> While your husband is gone, do one thing—preferably speaking his love language—that says, "I was thinking about you while you were away."

can't get to the phone at a reasonable hour, try setting
up an e-mail or fax system to stay in touch.

- *Think good thoughts.* It's important to change your
  thought process if you are angry your husband is
  gone. Keep in mind that most men don't enjoy traveling, so he's probably not having any more fun than
  you are. Never forget that you're a team and you each
  have a job to do. Try to concentrate on the fact that
  he is traveling to provide for you and the family and
  to support a lifestyle you've both chosen. Remember
  that the flip side of his travel could be unemployment.

- *Give grace.* When your child is sick and the water
  heater breaks, remind yourself, "The things that are
  inconveniencing me are not deliberate on his part."
  Gail says it really helps to give herself pep talks like
  "Rick did not make Katie get sick. He did not make the
  water heater break down."

- *Do one thing.* While your husband is gone, do one
  thing—preferably speaking his love language—that
  says, "I was thinking about you while you were
  away." This might include catching up on his ironing,
  wallpapering his study, or balancing the checkbook—
  whatever would let him know you were missing him.
  Not only will he feel drawn to you when he returns,
  but it will also help you regard him in a positive way.

- *Plan for re-entry.* Preparing to receive your husband
  back home is essential for making the transition
  smooth. Begin mentally preparing your children by
  telling them, "Daddy's coming home tonight!" Next,
  plan ahead for alone time for the two of you, as well
  as daddy-child time. If your kids are older, Gail recommends having your alone time when the kids are in
  school so they don't feel cheated.

We already know life will always upset that perfect balance of just the right amount of time together, so try not to be upset when you don't get it. Instead, bask in the luxury of those moments, planned or spontaneous, that reaffirm the caring passion and companionship you share with your husband. Since we love when those moments do occur, let's look at some ways we can increase the likelihood of them happening more often.

Physical Privacy

One morning, after teaching a marriage class based on the book *Creative Counterpart* by Linda Dillow, I spoke with Molly, who hesitantly told me that the physical aspect of her marriage wasn't all she'd hoped it would be. She and her husband didn't have any other critical issues, and neither had emotional baggage from previous relationships. They enjoyed lots of the same leisure activities, and she did the books for the business he ran. Her personality was easygoing and she didn't struggle with high expectations. Furthermore, both Molly and Jack made an effort to show their love for one another in meaningful ways. Overall, she said they had a great marriage, so she wasn't sure what the problem was.

As we talked a bit more I said, "Tell me about where you live." It turns out their fourteen-year-old son had the room right next to theirs, and both of their headboards shared the same wall.

The light went on, and I said, "Okay, Molly, here's your assignment for next week. Forget buying a sexy nightie [which was the homework for the rest of the class]. Instead, go home and rearrange the bedrooms. Move your five-year-old daughter into the room next to yours, and move your teenage son into your little girl's old bedroom at the end of the hall."

After sharing in detail the rest of the changes I wanted Molly to make, I said, "Let's talk next week after class to see if any of the suggestions I made helped."

The following week, Molly came up to me after class *glowing.* "Denise," she said, "I can't believe I never thought of switching the kids' bedrooms to give Jack and me more privacy! We had a wonderful week together."

Why is physical privacy a luxury? Linda Dillow once wrote, "We, in America, have been granted everything necessary to fully develop the talent of loving our men: we have privacy: a place to call our own where what is done in private is private."[5] Linda and her husband, Jody, served as missionaries for several years overseas in Europe and ministered in countries ravished by communism. Many of the women she met lived in tiny apartments, their entire families crammed into two rooms. If a bedroom even existed, the parents usually gave it to the children. I don't know one woman who lives in conditions even close to what our dear sisters endure in these underprivileged countries. Compared to the rest of the world, the homes we live in and our access to privacy is a luxury we sometimes take for granted.

Or, like my friend, Molly, we think we don't have privacy, when in reality it is something that is readily available to us.

Are You His Vacation Wife?

Vacations are definitely a luxury, aren't they? Whether you're flying to Hawaii for the first time or getting away to the mountains for a few days, a vacation is a luxury because you get a break from the stress, strain, and setting of normal everyday life. During the early years of our marriage, Stu used to frequently comment that I became a different woman when he took me away on vacation or for romantic overnight trips. Because of the floor plan of our house and the constant presence of four small children, I usually couldn't relax and enjoy my husband unless I was away from home.

When we lived in California, we had a thirty-seven-year-old, sixteen-hundred-square-foot house with cracker-thin walls. Our bedroom shared a common wall with our two little girls' room, and our two boys' room was less than three feet away. If my husband and I even *breathed* loud, our children heard. As you can imagine, our intimate moments together often were hampered by the knowledge our children could hear everything, even if at that age they didn't realize what was going on.

Also, since our home was older, no lock guarded the master bedroom door. So, before we'd make love, Stu would take a chair and shove it under the doorknob to make sure no little people could wander in. Of course, it now seems like a no-brainer—we should have just installed a new locking doorknob for our room. But I am not married to a handyman, and obviously, neither one of us was thinking clearly during those years.

Then God graciously moved us to Colorado. Our house has a floor plan where the master bedroom is situated apart from all the other bedrooms. We have no one beside us or below us. We don't share a wall with any of our kids' bedrooms, and we even have a lock on the door! My husband thought he'd died and gone to heaven because I finally became his "vacation wife" in the privacy of our own home.

Are you your husband's vacation wife at home? Or, like me, are you inhibited in your physical relationship with him out of fear of being overheard or the constant threat of interruptions? Privacy is essential to enhancing intimacy in your marriage. Let's take a moment to consider some ways you can ensure you and your husband have the privacy you need to make your marriage sizzle.

In the Bedroom

Make sure you have a lock on your bedroom door. Whether you have kids, houseguests, or friends who make themselves at home and walk right in, you'll be able to relax when you are with your lover. In the back of your mind you'll be secure in the knowledge that no one can come into your bedroom without your permission.

Next, if your bedroom shares a common wall with one of your children's, move the beds so your headboards are not against the same wall. Even better, position the beds in both rooms as far away from one another as possible. Like Molly, rearrange the furniture. You'll be amazed at how a few simple changes will create a greater sense of privacy.

> Just like an unwanted guest, the computer and television make their presence known and invade our personal space.

Finally, if it won't cause World War III, move the computer or television out of your bedroom if it infringes on the time you and your husband spend together. Modern technology is an often overlooked privacy buster. Just like an unwanted guest, the computer and television make their presence known and invade our personal space. It's hard to connect if you are focused on a talk show or he's visiting a newly updated Web site. If both of you are disciplined about these electronic wonders, they can stay. But often one spouse has a harder time than the other turning them off and keeping them off.

A thirtysomething wife named Tamara got her husband's attention and her point across in a cute way when she put a sticky note on the computer monitor. It read, "Turn me on instead of your computer." He eagerly complied, and after a sweet evening of togetherness, she was able to talk with him about feeling like a "computer widow" because of how much time he spent in front of the screen.

Because men are wired to have one-track minds, it's common for wives to feel shut out by them, whether it's the computer, the television, the newspaper, the latest bestseller, or even a musical instrument (Stu can get lost with his electric guitar for hours). Through prayer and discussion, work out a compromise you can both live with while maintaining pockets of privacy for the two of you in your bedroom.

Little Kids

When small children are at home, private time with your husband feels like the height of luxury. Now that our kids are older, Stu and I realize it was actually easier to have privacy when they were young. If you have little ones now, I know you're thinking, *That's impossible.* But let's look at some reasons it's usually simpler when they are young, and how you can find time alone for you and your hubby.

When your children are tiny babies, privacy isn't really an issue, because babies aren't old enough to be aware of much besides their hunger and comfort. Babies usually nap several hours a day and go to sleep early in the evening once they're a few months old. So you see, you really do have alone time with your husband, but you may just fall asleep on one another!

Toddlers are far more active and inquisitive, but again, they're probably in bed by seven or eight o'clock at night. I know some moms who tell me that their preschoolers don't go to bed until nine or ten; but you can change that (unless a genuine physical or psychological problem exists, of course). Like adults, children often need to "unwind" before they fall asleep. With this in mind we allowed for at least a half hour of down time with Mommy and Daddy, which included prayers, reading aloud and lots of snuggling. We also let our children take books to bed with them— board books when they were really little and less sturdy books when they were older. Bedtime was never an issue in our home because we learned over the years how to make it pleasant for all of us. Be creative in finding bedtime routines that will work for your family, and you may enjoy quiet evenings more often.

This is the time in life when you have to get intentional about scheduling your private moments together, or they can completely disappear. You might think, *That's so unromantic!* And, in a way, you're right. But even less romantic is a relationship put on hold indefinitely due to busyness. In some cases, a marriage won't survive, and in every case, your marriage certainly can't sizzle. So look at your calendar and be determined. Block out at least one night a week to be alone with your husband. And take heart; you should be able to add more afternoons or evenings as your kids get older and more independent.

> Block out at least one night a week to be alone with your husband.

Another tip is to take full advantage of the different times of the day or night when you do find yourselves alone. When your children are young, steal those moments when they're asleep during nap times. Or try going to bed when they do! You can always get up afterward, but retiring early with your husband to the privacy of your bedroom once in a while feels delicious.

School's In

Once your kids are school age, you'll have time alone when they're in class, unless you're home schooling. Invite your husband to meet you at home for lunch and dessert (you!). Do this every month or so, and he will love you for it. You'll find you feel better about your relationship too.

Never quit looking for those hours in your day the two of you could set aside for each other, then seize the moment!

Take a Nap

My husband was raised in a southern family where Sunday naps were mandatory. Besides his parents wanting to honor the concept of the Sabbath, I'm sure having seven children made Sunday naps more of a necessity than a luxury! When our children were young, they came home exhausted after a morning of Sunday school. We would eat lunch, then everyone would go to his or her respective room to nap. Now that our kids are teenagers and young adults, they're so used to Mom and Dad taking Sunday-afternoon naps, they don't give it a second thought. But they probably suspect we do more than sleep.

If you're a mother of young children, try introducing even short naps with your husband. That way when the kids are older, like ours, they're already used to the idea. If your kids are already older, you and your husband can still start a nap tradition—but don't be surprised if you get a few questioning stares from your teens.

Big Kids

Those snickers and knowing looks from teens bring me to my next point. Women with older children often tell me they're uncomfortable making love with their husbands unless all of their kids are out of the house or asleep. In our home, that means Stu and I would make love only between midnight and five o'clock in the morning! I don't know about you, but I don't want to be touched during the hours I'm supposed to be getting my beauty sleep.

Believe it or not, it's sometimes harder to find private time with your husband when your kids are older. On a recent weeknight, Susan and her husband decided to get romantic, but within forty-five minutes, their older, at-home kids interrupted them four times. If you have young adults at home who have jobs and are in college, you know their schedules are crazy.

At our house, each one of our kids likes to check in with us when they come in for the night. Unless it's midnight on a Friday or Saturday, once they're in the door, the first stop is our bedroom to tell us all about whatever they did that night. I'm thrilled our teens still like to talk to us, but it has made lovemaking a little tricky at times. It's especially disconcerting for me, since they now know where babies come from and what married couples do.

> Although we might consider dates a luxury because they are, to quote our earlier definition, "an enjoyment usually considered unnecessary to life or health," experts agree dates are essential to the life and health of a close, loving marriage.

We all agree it can hinder intimate, romantic times with your husband when you realize your teenager knows what you're doing. Yikes! That's enough to make some moms call a halt right there. But just as you need to get intentional about making time for each other when life speeds up, mothers of older children may need to adjust their outlook for the sake of intimacy with their husbands. If physical fatigue is an obstacle to you when kids are younger, your attitude can be just as much a hindrance when they're older. In reality, one of the greatest gifts we can give our children is a healthy perspective on the physical joys of marriage.

Kelley's husband is an artist who works out of their home.

Kelley is the mother of five older children. One day during summer vacation, when all five kids were running in and out of the house, Kelley realized it had been too long since she and her honey had spent some intimate time together. Kelley took a deep breath and invited her husband to take a shower (and more) with her in the middle of the day. After he got over the shock, he gladly joined her and loved it. She said it was all he could talk about for weeks. Kelley told me she actually enjoyed herself once she got into the moment. But first, she had to readjust her mind-set and decide to put her relationship with Gary over her need to feel comfortable.

No matter what stage of life you're in, you must allow yourself to be stretched and pushed out of your comfort zone if you truly desire to maintain a close and intimate relationship with your husband.

Mini Luxuries: Dates

Dates are great when you're getting to know one another, aren't they? The phone rings and the man you hoped to hear from is on the line, asking you to go somewhere and do something with him. Once you're married, this fun can continue, but your time together can end on an even more romantic note than a goodnight kiss at the front door of your house.

Although we might consider dates a luxury because they are, to quote our earlier definition, "an enjoyment usually considered unnecessary to life or health," experts agree dates are essential to the life and health of a close, loving marriage.

Once you're married, what do you *do* on your dates? In the preceding chapter I talked about the different seasons of married life and how to be your husband's recreational companion through the years. Dating your husband can follow the same flow. Depending on the life phase you're in, your dates may look different this year than they will five years from now.

Dave and Claudia Arp, in their fun book titled *52 Dates for You and Your Mate*, divide dates for married couples into several categories taking into account budgets, life stages, and even energy levels. The authors wrote about actual dates real-life couples had gone on, ranging from the "Bland Date" to chartering a sailboat with two other couples for a week in the crystal blue waters of the Caribbean!

> Unless you intentionally carve out time for a date with your spouse and then make sure it happens, it probably won't.

The "Bland Date" made me laugh. After several stressful months, this particular couple learned one of them had an ulcer and needed to follow a bland diet. So, they decided to devote an entire evening to "blandness." They both wore beige clothes and ate chicken, white rice, baked apples, and vanilla ice cream. They also listened to really slow music that brought their mood down.[6] What impressed me most about this couple is how they took a discouraging moment in their marriage and turned it into a creative memory.

For most of us, dates with our husbands will fall somewhere between these two extremes. As with everything else we've mentioned so far, unless you intentionally carve out time for a date with your spouse and then make sure it happens, it probably won't.

When children are small or work schedules overload you, you may not have a lot of time or energy left to get superimaginative on a date. If that's where you and your husband are right now, take a few minutes tonight or on the phone today to brainstorm three dates you'd each like to take in the next three months. They can be as simple as ordering take-out Chinese food and renting a video or enjoying a barbecue in your own backyard after the kids have been put to bed. (If you do this second date, make sure you've got appetizers to munch on so neither one of you gets cranky due to eating dinner later.)

If you're at a point in life where circumstances are a little easier and you have some breathing room in your time and finances, each of you should list at least one "dream date" you'd like. Once you have an idea of what your husband desires, be a great wife and take the first step by planning his dream date. Even though most of us long to be swept off our feet by an incredibly romantic date arranged by our husbands, if we want a marriage that sizzles, we have to realize the responsibility may fall on us at times to create the romantic atmosphere we crave.

> We have to realize the responsibility may fall on us at times to create the romantic atmosphere we crave.

Instead of getting discouraged because you have to jump-start the sizzle in your marriage, ask the Lord to help you have a good attitude and put some effort into making your husband feel loved. Generally, those good feelings your date generates will also spill over to you. If you take a step in the direction of moving your relationship toward intimacy and passion, hopefully, your husband will realize the benefits and do his part too.

Once, Stu planned a date for the entire day. We began by shopping together for a bedroom set. Shopping isn't high on

Stu's list of fun things to do, but he knows how much I like to look for big-ticket items with him. We ate lunch at a delightful little restaurant. Afterward, Stu surprised me and took me to a Thomas Kinkade gallery.

That was one of those perfect days in marriage we all wish could take place more often. I felt so loved and cared for because Stu placed my preferences and pleasure over his. Ideally, a husband and wife should take turns having favorite dates if their tastes differ. But if you and your husband enjoy the same things, you won't have to try as hard to have fun together. Remember, whatever works best for the two of you and increases the joy and emotional and physical closeness in your marriage is what matters.

Married dates are so much better than dates when you're single because you have the luxury of God's blessing to enjoy your physical relationship to the fullest. To be able to consummate the laughter, secrets shared, and the memories you've just made on your date by expressing your love sexually is one of God's most beautiful gifts to a husband and wife. Don't leave out the perfect ending to a perfect evening or day spent in the company of one another. It could be the most precious part of your time together.

The Ultimate Luxury

The ultimate in privacy and luxury is getting away as a couple for the sole purpose of relaxing and enjoying each other. These getaways can be for a night or two, or longer if your time and budget allow. You can even plan a romantic escape in your own home, especially if you have friends or family you can swap watching children with for a weekend. But, in order for an at-home rendezvous to be a success, you both have to be disciplined about letting things go around the house and not answering the phone.

Depending on how long your getaway is, try not to fill up your time with too much shopping and sightseeing, unless this is a priority to both of you. Instead, let this be a sweet time of concentrating on each other and rediscovering the spark in your relationship that drew you together in the first place. Think about bringing your wedding album if it's an anniversary getaway, or buy new lingerie and undergarments for both of you, if your escape is to celebrate a birthday.

To help your conversations go deeper than they might otherwise, go to your local Christian bookstore and buy a book with specific questions married couples can ask one another. (Look in the back of this book for sample conversation starters. If you and your husband have a lot of catching up to do, start with the less threatening questions.) If all goes well, you'll both feel free to open up to each other as you spend more time together.

Dan and Beth took off in their trailer for a camping trip as their weekend away. They hiked a different trail every day, played Scrabble in the evenings, and enjoyed romantic candlelight dinners at local restaurants. Dan said it was one of the best weekends he's ever had with Beth. They both came back in love, refreshed, and ready to face the rat race of everyday life.

If either of you likes surprises, one of you can do all the planning and kidnap the other. Just make sure you both have everything you need for an unforgettable weekend. Because of work and other logistics, a surprise getaway may not be an option. That's okay. Many times anticipating a weekend away is as much fun as the actual trip! Knowing you have a mini trip with your hubby to look forward to can get you through mountains of laundry and hectic deadlines.

When I give my "Sizzle" talk, I'm amazed at the number of wives who tell me their men ask them to go away all the time, but these women won't leave their jobs, dogs, or children. And when I say children, I'm not talking about nursing babies. Their kids are sleeping through the night, usually potty trained, and many are already school age. Shame on us! We need to be grateful our husbands want us to join them on their latest business trip or skiing adventure. My advice to these gals is, GO!! Leave the kids (or animals) with people you trust, and make the man in your life happy. Even though you love your children with all your heart, don't let them become an excuse not to love your husband.

One year, when our kids were little, Stu decided he wanted to go away with me for a weekend to Monterey Bay for his birthday. Because we had so many children, we hired two older teenage girls from our church to watch them. Our weekend was wonderful—a great time of reconnecting, relaxing, and exploring this seaside community. When we arrived home, our two sitters met us at the door with open arms. They were thrilled to see us and return the care of our little ones to us.

> Even though you love your children with all your heart, don't let them become an excuse not to love your husband.

I asked, "Well, how did it go?"

They replied, "Mr. and Mrs. Vezey, we don't see how you do it. Please don't get mad, but by dinnertime Saturday we were so exhausted, we set all of your clocks ahead an hour and told the kids it was time for bed at eight o'clock, when it was really only seven!"

We all enjoyed a good laugh, and I was glad I picked up

something extra for them. I share this story with you to encourage you that no one died, everyone survived, and our marriage thrived because I chose to go away with my husband instead of stay home with the kids.

I hope you'll do the same.

LIBERATED FOR LOVE

You will know the truth, and the truth will set you free.

John 8:32

C aroline sat across from me and wept. Her shoulders shook as tears spilled down her cheeks. "Denise," she said, her voice quavering, "I want intimacy and passion in my marriage. I want all the things with my husband you talked about this morning, but something must be wrong with me. I don't really feel close to my husband or enjoy sexual relations with him like I know I should. I think it's because ..."

Almost every time I give the "Secrets to Make Your Marriage Sizzle" talk, this scene is reenacted. The reasons a woman might give for disliking sex or avoiding emotional closeness with her husband vary, but the common denominator is heartache and pain. Many precious women have been cut so deeply by the knife-sharp circumstances of life. On the outside, these wives are trying desperately to honor the biblical mandates for marriage, but inside, their hearts are torn and bleeding.

If you've read this far and can't relate to what I'm describing, please don't skip over this chapter. You are a fortunate woman if the cutting edge of pain hasn't ripped a portion of the fabric of your life. But I'm sure you know *someone* who does need what is written here. It may be a coworker, a girlfriend, your sister, or even your own daughter. Virtually every woman in our culture has been touched—or knows someone who has been impacted—by either the emotional trauma stemming from sexual abuse or the physical consequences and intense spiritual conflict due to immoral behavior.

If you find yourself in one of these situations, the information in this chapter might be overwhelming for you. Some of the ladies who have reviewed this material with me in the past suggest reading through the prayers and materials with a trusted friend or mentor—one who can help you work through any upsetting emotions that may surface. My prayer for you is that as you walk with other women who will share your pain, you will discover the liberating truth of Secret 5: Jesus Christ wants to set you free for love.

Secret 5

Would you like to look forward to times of physical intimacy with your husband? Have you always known that there had to be something more to this God-given gift of sexual intercourse than you're experiencing? Maybe you and your spouse are compatible physically, but what's missing is a strong undercurrent of emotional connectedness. Let's look at some key areas that need the intervention of Jesus Christ and His Holy Spirit in our lives to promote healing and to create the loving, healthy marriage relationship we all desire.

Baggage from the Past

Unfortunately, our generation has the shameful distinction of flagrantly breaking with the moral guidelines that used to govern our society and most individuals. The previous generation was the last one in which most persons adhered to strict moral teachings, even if an individual wasn't a Christian. Less than forty years ago, engaging in a sexual relationship without benefit of marriage was frowned on; having a child outside of marriage was scandalous. In fact, the humiliation was so great, girls were usually sent away during their pregnancies and didn't reenter society until their babies had been given up for adoption.

We know this isn't the case today. In our sex-saturated culture, unmarried couples living together is so common the U.S. Census Bureau says this arrangement makes up 9 percent (or 4.9 million) of the households in America.[1] Even more unsettling is the 26 percent who are single mothers, raising children without fathers.[2]

Because of this moral shift, many women enter marriage with emotional, spiritual, and sometimes physical baggage from past relationships. Sometimes they chose heavy petting or intercourse with their boyfriends. Other times they went even further outside the boundaries and experimented with different sexual lifestyles or promiscuity. And for those women who felt they had no other choice but to abort an unborn child, a lifetime doesn't seem long enough to erase the agonizing guilt and ongoing torment caused by knowing they ended their child's life.

> Our first baby step on the path to freedom is asking God's forgiveness for the sinful choices that defiled us and kept us from God's highest will of staying sexually pure until marriage.

How can we respond to these mountains of pain? To begin with, we are going to praise God that in Him we are forgiven from the past and can find the freedom we so desperately need.

The Lord tells us in Isaiah 61:1 that He has sent His Spirit to "bind up the brokenhearted, to proclaim freedom for the captives and release from darkness for the prisoners." If God has promised something, I don't want to settle for anything less.

The Healing Journey

Our first baby step on the path to freedom is asking God's forgiveness for the sinful choices that defiled us and kept us from God's highest will of staying sexually pure until marriage. If you have not done this yet or don't remember if you have, please take a moment right now and ask the Lord to forgive you for sinning against Him in this way. It can be a simple prayer. What matters to God is that we have a heart of repentance, which comes only from a sincere realization that in failing to keep our bodies only for our husbands, we sinned against the Lord and our mates.

Along these same lines, the next step is forgiving the partner or partners we were sexually involved with. Many women have shared that they didn't really want to be so physically involved with past boyfriends, but they felt pressured into becoming sexually active or they feared they would lose the relationship if they didn't. I'm not saying this justifies our actions, but it explains why so many women crossed a line they never intended to.

Again, this can be a simple prayer. Notice I said simple, not necessarily easy. Our thoughts and emotions can be a powerful force in resisting a straightforward command. Nevertheless, Christ asks us to forgive others as we ourselves would like to be forgiven.[3] We may even need to extend this forgiveness to our own husbands. Many wives went too far physically with their husbands before they married. Even if you were engaged, God still does not condone sex outside the marriage relationship (Deut. 22:23–24). If your husband seems open to the idea, you might share with him the importance of seeking forgiveness from God and each other, and ask if he is willing to pray with you.

You may also find it helpful to write a note or letter to the person you are forgiving. Whether or not you actually send it is a personal decision to be made only after much prayer and wise counsel. Whatever you choose to do, the very act of writing is healing in many ways. It can help you clarify your thoughts and express your feelings more fully; also, it gives you a written record of what and whom you forgave, as well as the intentions of your heart, should you ever doubt the sincerity of your forgiveness.

Deeper Streams

Further along this same pathway is our need to ask the Lord's mercy and forgiveness if we have had an abortion. My heart goes out to those women who face this pain daily. If you are one of them, I want to stop right now and encourage you with this beautiful word from God: "Nothing in all creation will ever be able to separate us from the love of God that is revealed in Christ Jesus our Lord" (Rom. 8:39 NLT). *Nothing!* Not any sin we've committed, not any trouble we face, no evil done against us, not Satan's worst snares. Nothing will keep God from loving us, reaching out to us, and caring for us when we are connected to Him through Jesus Christ.

> Nothing will keep God from loving us, reaching out to us, and caring for us when we are connected to Him through Jesus Christ.

Even if the father of the baby you aborted was your husband, please don't let anything keep you both from humbly approaching God and asking His forgiveness. Whether you acted out of ignorance or with full knowledge, you can experience restoration, peace, and even joy.

I understand this is a terribly short section on a highly emotional and complex issue. Therefore, if you or someone you know would like more in-depth counsel for this sensitive area, I've included a list of resources at the end of this book that may be of help to you.

Roadblocks

As we continue on our journey, one of the greatest hindrances to healing is the failure to forgive ourselves. We tend to believe Satan's lies and our own negative self-talk: "I am unworthy; I'm unlovable; I'm too bad."

> If you have genuinely asked God's forgiveness for all you remember concerning your sexual past, every deed you participated in is completely erased.

No matter what your feelings say, you are precious to God. That cannot be expressed strongly enough. Here is a truth we can anchor ourselves to: "If we confess our sins to him, he can be depended on to forgive us and to cleanse us from every wrong," (1 John 1:9 TLB). If you have genuinely asked God's forgiveness for all you remember concerning your sexual past, every deed you participated in is completely erased. You are as clean and spotless in His eyes as a fresh, untouched canvas awaiting the artist's hand.

When you are plagued by recriminating thoughts, here are some uplifting truths from God's Word to encourage you:

When I feel	What is true	Why it is true
Unworthy and unacceptable	I am accepted and worthy.	Rom. 15:7; Ps. 139
Depressed and hopeless	I have all the hope I need.	Rom. 15:13; Ps. 16:11; 27:13
Imperfect/not good enough.	I am perfect in Jesus.	Heb. 10:14; Col. 2:13
In bondage	I am free in Jesus.	Ps. 32:7; 2 Cor. 3:17; John 8:36
Guilty	I am totally forgiven and redeemed.	Ps. 103:12; Eph. 1:7; Col. 1:14; Heb. 10:17
Unloved	I am loved.	John 15:9; Eph. 2:4; 5:1; 1 John 4:10
Condemned	I am blameless.	John 3:18; Rom. 8:1
I cannot reach God	I have direct access to God.	Eph. 2:6; 1 Peter 2:5, 9

If you have been battling thoughts like those in column one, this is a good resting place in the journey. Stop and praise God for the complete forgiveness we have in Him and for the emotional, spiritual, and physical freedom He alone can provide.

Physical Detours

Another distressing problem from the past that can potentially affect the sizzle with your husband today is sexually transmitted disease. Some women, and men, carry the physical repercussions of their sexual encounters for the rest of their lives. Several women I've met with have said the herpes virus they contracted dictates their sexual relations with their husbands to this day. Even more sobering are the anguished stories of close calls when children are born while the virus is active, or the sad stories of

wives contracting sexually transmitted diseases from their formerly promiscuous husbands.

I'm not a doctor and therefore not qualified to discuss the
latest treatments available for the variety of STDs ravaging our
culture. My heart breaks with yours, however, if the physical
repercussions of an immoral past are quenching the fire of a passionate relationship today. If these conditions exist in your
marriage, I hope you and your husband have already consulted
a physician and are doing everything possible to maximize your
health. Try not to be discouraged. Hope and healing for both of
you can still be found with treatment and through the Lord. But
you may need to adjust your expectations and let go of the ideal
you once held for your sexual relationship with your husband.

The Heart of the Matter

For some women reading this, forgiveness and physical healing
still aren't enough to mend what is missing in their emotional
and sexual relationships with their husbands. What else is
there? The answer lies in how God has wired us physically, emotionally, and spiritually.

> There's more to sex than mere skin on skin. Sex is as
> much spiritual mystery as physical fact. As written in
> Scripture, "The two become one." ... we must not pursue
> the kind of sex that avoids commitment and intimacy,
> leaving us more lonely than ever—the kind of sex that
> can never "become one." ... In sexual sin we violate the
> sacredness of our own bodies, these bodies that were
> made for God-given and God-modeled love, for "becom-
> ing one" with another. (1 Cor. 6:16–18 MSG)

John and Paula Sanford, long-time Christian counselors and
co-authors of several books, have this to say about those verses:

> God has created husbands and wives to become one
> flesh in holy union according to Genesis 2:24 and

Ephesians 5:31, "and a man shall leave his father and his mother and shall be joined to his wife, and the two shall become one flesh." When two become one flesh in a holy union, their spirits reach out and latch on to one another because this is what they were created to do. Men and women who have been involved with fornication (sex outside of marriage) and adultery (sex when one or both of the partners are married to other people) meet in sinful perversion of God's intent. They have not been given his permission (to be joined in sexual union) and blessing in marriage, but it does not prevent their spirits from reaching out and latching on to one another, because this is what we were created to do.[4]

Every time you have sexual intercourse or intimate physical contact outside of the God-ordained state of marriage, not just your bodies and emotions are involved. Your spirit is also affected. The truth behind the verse "the two shall become one" is that not only will your flesh be united as one, but your minds, emotions, and spirits will be as well, *whether you intend for them to or not!* Your spirit may still be tied to individuals you had sexual encounters with, even if emotionally and physically you are no longer connected to those people.

> The truth behind the verse "the two shall become one" is that not only will your flesh be united as one, but your minds, emotions, and spirits will be as well

I realize this may be a difficult teaching to understand. If I hadn't seen such success in helping women be set free to love their husbands with an undivided heart and spirit, I wouldn't have included it. But since I have, I felt compelled to share this little-known concept with you.

With this in mind, read over this list of markers to help determine if a sexual experience in either your or your husband's past negatively impacts your marriage today.

- *An unsatisfactory physical relationship.* If either of you was promiscuous or sexually active and find the physical monogamy of marriage boring, this could be an indicator of incomplete healing and a need for spiritual separation of past relationships.
- *Recurring dreams of past lovers, even one-night stands.*
- *A continuing emotional attraction or idealizing of a previous relationship.* This phenomenon is common and explains how couples who haven't seen each other for years can meet again and instantly reconnect, even if they are both in committed, stable marriages.

Sheila is a good example of a wife who experienced these spirit ties and had no idea what was happening or why. A devoted wife and loving mother, she couldn't understand why she didn't really enjoy physical relations with her husband and, even more disturbing, why she frequently dreamed of a former boyfriend she cared nothing about. Sheila had asked God's forgiveness for going too far with this guy in high school, but he still invaded her dreams at night.

I assured Sheila she wasn't alone. The wonderful news is that with God's help you, too, can break the spiritual chains that hold you to your former life.

Your Map and Guide

If you're going somewhere you've never gone before, you wouldn't think of starting out without a road map unless you were traveling with someone who knew the route and offered to be your guide. This next section contains several prayers that can serve as road maps on your journey to healing. Best of all, the Holy Spirit will be your guide, completely available to lead and help, so you don't have to make this journey alone.

What follows are some general instructions for all of the prayers: To begin with, be sure you pray aloud. In addition, make sure you go through a prayer separately for each person you were involved with. Also, if you sincerely pray and don't notice any difference in your life, you may want to invite a godly and mature friend or mentor to pray with you. Jesus promised us in Matthew 18:19–20, "If two of you on earth agree about anything you ask for, it will be done for you by my Father in heaven. For where two or three come together in my name, there am I with them." Sometimes, especially if a powerful bond exists from a previous relationship, it helps to have another believer praying with you.

This first prayer is to break all spiritual ties with anyone you chose to have sexual contact with outside of marriage. This includes any homosexual liaisons as well. If you committed sexual sin with your husband, leave out any sentences regarding "breaking the spiritual union," "granting spiritual freedom," and "returning my spirit to me." You *want* to feel strongly tied to your husband, not disconnected.

The first time I taught this material at a Bible study for wives, it changed the lives of two women forever because they chose to recognize and believe these prayers might be of help to them.

Barb was an outspoken type A kind of woman. When I mentioned I would be available to pray after the class with anyone who wanted to, she jumped out of her seat and was the first in line. We walked over to a secluded section of the sanctuary, and the story of her life before Christ spilled out with each heart-wrenching repetition of the prayer.

"Lord, forgive me and separate me from all of the men who were my boyfriends [she listed six in all] that I repeatedly had sexual relations with." "Lord, forgive me and separate my spirit from _____ who I lived with for ten months." "Lord, forgive me and separate my spirit from _____ and _____, the couple I had a ménage a trois with." "Lord, forgive me for having a lesbian encounter with_____."

At one point, Barb looked up at me, her eyes swollen and red from tears, and cried, "I'm so embarrassed, I'm so embarrassed." I gently put my arms around her and said, "Barb, Satan wants you to be embarrassed because he doesn't want you to be free. He wants to keep you chained to these past lovers and feeling forever condemned, to keep you from all God has for you, and from being the woman He desires for you to be, one who brings Him glory and is useful in His kingdom."

> Satan wants you to be embarrassed because he doesn't want you to be free.

Barb continued praying through her list, until everyone she had ever been intimate with was covered. We hugged when she finished, and Barb told me she felt as if a thousand-pound boulder had just rolled off her shoulders. Praise God.

Rita, who was actually Barb's best friend, was the polar opposite of Barb. A quiet, poised, and calm woman, Rita had a natural beauty that shone from her unadorned face. As I taught that day, I had no idea who needed the concepts I shared. However, the next morning I received a phone call from Rita.

"Denise," she began, "when you offered to pray with us in class, I thought about it for a minute, but I was too embarrassed to have other women know I even needed any of those prayers. But I did go home and pray out loud through each boyfriend I had before Frank [her husband]. There were really only two, but

I did go all the way with them. I didn't tell Frank what I'd prayed; I just called him on his cell phone and told him I'd be waiting up for him when he got home.

"That night, I put on a sexy nightie he'd given me a while ago. You should have seen his face light up when he realized I'd waited up for *that!* It was the *best* night we've ever had. When we were finished, Frank looked at me and said, 'Wow, what happened?' So I told him about our class and praying through the prayer to be separated from my old boyfriends. He gave me the biggest hug and said how happy he was and also asked if he could go through the prayer for a former girlfriend he'd been with sexually.

"Denise, for the first time I felt completely free from my past when we made love. No ghosts of previous lovers overshadowed what my husband and I shared. Thank you, thank you, thank you."

If you need to pray this prayer, may you sense the Lord's presence and His pleasure as you move forward on the next part of your journey.

Prayer of Separation for Sexual Contact Outside of Marriage

Dear heavenly Father,

I know that it was sinful and offensive to You when I committed sexual immorality by (name the offense) with (name of person). I understand that by this sexual act I joined my spirit together with _____'s spirit. I ask that You forgive me for (the offense) and that You will break this spiritual union with _____. Grant me spiritual freedom from _____ and return my spirit to me. I ask that the blood of Jesus would cleanse my spirit as it returns to me. I pray that the door of sensual thought and action toward _____ would be closed forever. Dear God, make me spiritually whole again. I pray this by faith and through the power of Jesus Christ. Amen.[5]

Am I Having an Affair?

This same prayer can be used with a few changes if you have formed an emotional attachment to someone other than your husband. In the Christian community, this is more common than physical affairs because we can feel we haven't "crossed the line" and committed actual adultery. But according to Jesus' words, this isn't true. He warned us in the book of Matthew, "You know the next commandment pretty well, too: 'Don't go to bed with another's spouse.' But don't think you've preserved your virtue simply by staying out of bed. Your *heart* can be corrupted by lust even quicker than your body. Those leering looks you think nobody notices—they also corrupt" (5:27–28 MSG).

> Your heart can be corrupted by lust even quicker than your body.

As women, we don't tend to become attracted to someone for the physical aspect alone. The other man is usually meeting an emotional need that your husband isn't filling to your satisfaction. Maybe he has excellent manners, always opens the door for you, or pleasantly asks how you are. Perhaps he's sensitive, a good listener, and participates in your conversations like he really *heard* what you said. If he's a coworker, you might respect how he handles his job or other matters at work compared to your more laid-back husband.

One Sunday morning at church, I nonchalantly asked a neighbor how she was doing. That two-minute interaction turned into an hour-long confessional. We found an empty room, and Tricia told me that she was contemplating leaving her husband for another man, someone from work. A man who called himself a Christian, I might add. It had started out innocently enough. They met getting coffee, then learned they were assigned to the same project. But things turned a corner one day when Tricia, upset over a confrontation with her husband, Jeff, confided her troubles to David.

David was sympathetic, understanding, and ready. He was attracted to Tricia and wasted no time letting her know. "You're a beautiful woman," he said. "You deserve better than Jeff. I've had feelings for you for a long time, Tricia. Let's go for dinner after work so we can talk."

Doesn't this conversation remind you of the one Eve had with the serpent at the Tree of the Knowledge of Good and Evil right before she ate the fruit? You know the rest of the story. The characters are different, the forbidden fruit is not the same, but Satan uses the same tactics and persuasive arguments. He feeds our sense of entitlement and gets us to fall away from the best-laid plans of God for our lives.

> The characters are different, the forbidden fruit is not the same, but Satan uses the same tactics and persuasive arguments.

If you find yourself constantly thinking of a man other than your husband and looking for opportunities to run into him, if you are putting extra thought into what you'll wear or how you'll look when you know you are going to see him, if you are manipulating situations so you can talk to him or confiding personal matters that should stay between you and your husband—run, don't walk, away. As far as you can, as fast as you can.

Tricia was a wise woman. I am so proud of her! After our meeting, she requested a transfer out of the office where she and

David worked. The next time David called, she told him she couldn't talk to him anymore. Tricia let him know she felt convicted to save her marriage. After that, she changed her cell phone number. (David never called her at home, for obvious reasons.)

Today, Tricia and Jeff are happier than ever. Instead of hiding what happened, Tricia confessed to Jeff how close she came to being unfaithful, and together they honestly discussed what problems in their marriage drove her even to think of another man in the first place. To his credit, Jeff asked Tricia's forgiveness and began addressing the issues she was most concerned about.

When Tricia and I sat together that Sunday, I had her pray this adapted version of the separation of spirits prayer to help break her attraction to David.

Prayer of Separation for Emotional Attachment

Dear heavenly Father,

I know that it is sinful and offensive to You when I fill my heart and mind with immoral thoughts about (name of person). I understand that by dwelling on him, I have opened a door, and my spirit is reaching out to _____'s spirit.

I ask that You forgive me for finding delight and emotional satisfaction in _____ and that You will break this spiritual union with him. Grant me spiritual freedom from _____ and return my spirit, thoughts, and heart to me. I ask that the blood of Jesus would cleanse my spirit as it returns to me. I pray that the door of sensual thought and action toward _____ would be closed forever.

Dear God, make me spiritually whole again and completely devoted to my spouse, (name of spouse). I pray this by faith and through the power of Jesus Christ. Amen.[6]

A word of caution: Just praying this prayer will not be

enough. You will probably need to pray it several times, perhaps daily, depending on how strong the attachment is, until you begin to sense a measure of freedom. Furthermore, you must take action and break off contact with whomever you are attracted to. Walk a different way to the water cooler. Change Sunday school classes. Get a different contractor to finish the remodel on your house. I *know* this seems extreme, but the battle for your marriage is just that—a battle—and it's one you can't afford to lose.

Divorced Legally, Not Spiritually

No one ever gets married intending to divorce. Actually, in the secular world that's only partially true; it's what most prenuptial agreements are about. Divorce is not the unforgivable sin, but I believe we treat it far more lightly than the Bible says we ought. Paul, in his letter to the Ephesians, compared the marriage relationship to Christ's commitment to, sacrifice for, and intimacy with the church.[7] The biblical grounds for divorce are few and strict. In fact, they are much narrower than the parameters most of us have accepted today.

If you or someone you know is contemplating divorce, I pray you will do everything possible to keep the relationship together. Begin by seeking God and His strength with your whole heart so you can stand before Him and know you did all He asked of you in this relationship. Next, surround yourself with mature, godly women who will support you and yet not take up an offense against your husband. Find a good Christian counselor or go to your pastor to help you and your husband negotiate rough waters. Even if your husband won't go with you, get the help you need from experts. Read books pertaining to your situation and, most important, pray against the Enemy of our souls, who wants nothing more than to see Christian marriages destroyed. And when you've done all this, go back to the beginning and seek God again on behalf of your marriage. I do need to qualify these guidelines by saying if you are in a dangerous marriage due to abuse, drug use, or alcohol addiction, it may be necessary to physically separate and then go through the steps outlined above.

Divorce is serious. It is more than just two people deciding to go their separate ways. It's an actual death. The relationship dies, and so do the dreams a couple once shared. It is also the death of that particular family unit and of all God had planned for you as husband and wife.

As with any death, grief is inevitable—heartbreaking grief. Grieving is the long, slow, painful process of learning to live again, in this case without the lifemate you once had. No quick fixes are offered for the newly divorced, although some individuals mistakenly believe a different partner right away will mend the hurt in their soul.

I hope you'll agree that your marriage is a life worth saving. The sad reality is that often only one partner wants the relationship to work, and while it takes two to marry, it only takes one to divorce. If you are divorced, this next prayer is written to help further the healing process. As with the other prayers, this one addresses what needs to take place in your spirit to enable you to move forward. This prayer should be prayed only when absolutely no possibility or opportunity for reconciliation between spouses remains.

Prayer of Separation for Divorced Persons

Dear heavenly Father,

I pray that You would forgive me for my part in the destruction of my marriage to (name of person). I know that the Bible says You hate divorce. I know that our divorce was sinful and offensive to You. I ask that You forgive me for breaking the vows I made to _____. I forgive _____ for not being faithful to the marriage vows we made before You. I understand that by our sexual

union in marriage, I became spiritually one with
_____. Because of this divorce, I ask that You break
this spiritual union with _____, grant me spiritual
freedom from _____, and return my spirit to me. I ask
that the precious blood of Jesus would cleanse my spirit as
it returns to me. I pray that the door of sensual thought
and action toward _____ will be forever closed. Dear
God, please make me spiritually whole again. This I pray
by faith and through the power of Jesus Christ. Amen.[8]

As your spirit begins to heal, hopefully you will notice your
heart and emotions becoming whole as well. Jesus said He came
that we "might have life, and might have it abundantly" (John
10:10 NASB). I pray this will be true for you.

Friend of a Wounded Heart

Wayne Watson wrote a song several years ago that I still love.
The title describes Jesus as "The Friend of a Wounded Heart."
This final prayer is written specifically for those precious
women who have been traumatized by sexual abuse. I don't
believe a woman can bear a deeper wound than the one that
comes from being forced or enticed against her will to engage
in sexual acts reserved only for the privacy and sacredness of a
loving marriage.

One of the greatest heartaches many abused women are left
with is an inability to fully enjoy sexual relations within the
context of marriage. If this describes you, and you have gotten
this far into the book because you desire to make your marriage
sizzle, please know I appreciate how difficult the preceding
chapters may have been for you. You *want* the intimacy and passion you've read about, but at the same time, powerful
memories and scarred emotions prevent you from experiencing
complete joy in some aspects of your relationship with your
husband.

No formula or one-time answer can bring healing and

restoration to the sexually abused. The survivor simply must take steps—big and small—toward greater freedom physically, emotionally, and spiritually. We all begin at the same point on our journey toward healing in our spirits—the place of forgiveness. But as we travel farther on, our paths diverge depending on the direction we need to take. If you do not need the guidelines that follow, I hope you will take the time to read through them to gain compassion for the many women whose lives have been fractured by abuse.

Although no woman consents to molestation, a bond was formed in the spiritual realm because the bodies that house the spirits of the abused and the abuser were intimately joined. Psychologists have noted that if someone is sexually abused by a member of the same sex, it greatly increases the probability of that individual becoming homosexual.[9] Secular psychology seems to be confirming what many Christians believe to be true: A spiritual bond has occurred that is influencing these lives.

We often like to take care of the difficulties in our lives by first addressing physical needs, then emotional issues, and finally, if we haven't gotten the results we're seeking, spiritual answers. As we pursue our restoration, we're going to change this order. Let's begin with our spirits, which are often neglected even in Christian circles. Then, like pebbles tossed upon still waters, I pray rings of healing will radiate from the center.

For those women who have been sexually molested by their fathers, it may be too painful to pray the following prayer using the term "Father." If this is true, try substituting a name of God that helps you personally feel close to Him. You may wish to call Him your Redeemer, Savior, Lamb of God, Wonderful Counselor, Mighty God, or Prince of Peace. Be assured, God loves us to call Him by one of His many names. He takes great delight in knowing you feel able to come to Him.

Many abuse victims struggle with wondering why God allowed such evil to happen in the first place; after all, He is all-powerful and could have prevented it. This line of thinking goes even further back to why God created a world where any suffering occurs at all. Without minimizing the incredible pain of abuse and all the other atrocities that are perpetrated here on earth, I hope you will discover the peace to be found in knowing *nothing* has touched our lives that is beyond God's power to redeem for good. May you also find rest in knowing that your abuser and all who have committed evil acts against others will be held accountable for their sins.[10] Praise God that He is just and no one will escape His judgment, even if by His mercy they have found salvation.

Prayer of Deliverance and Separation for Sexual Abuse Survivors

Dear heavenly Father,

I thank You that I am Your child, and because of Christ's blood shed for me, I am forgiven of all my sins and completely pure in Your eyes. You know I was sexually abused by (name or role of offender—e.g., babysitter, neighbor, and so forth—if name is not known) and that I hated it, but You know it also provided sexual stimulation. You also know it produced a certain guilt, almost as if I had asked for what happened, but I now recognize that is a lie. I was a victim, and I was not responsible for what was done to me.

God, by Your Holy Spirit, I choose to forgive my abuser(s). It's so hard to do, but I forgive them because You ask me to, Jesus. Please cleanse me from all sexual sins that have resulted from the demonic powers of lust, confusion, fear, and anger that have flourished in my life because of what took place in the past. Thank You, Lord, for forgiving me.

In the powerful name of Jesus Christ, I come against

every demonic power of lust, sexual perversion, fear, confusion, anger, shame, death, or any satanic power in the sexual realm that has been attached to my life as the result of what took place. I have confessed my sins to God, and He has forgiven me. As a child of God, reigning with Christ our Lord who defeated the Devil and all his company, you no longer have any grounds in my life. I command you, all of you demonic influences, to get out of my life. Go right now. You cannot hurt me as you go. You must go to where Jesus sends you, and do not return.

Thank You, Father, that those powers are leaving now. I choose to close the doors to them. May Your Spirit fill those areas of my life that have been influenced or controlled by these evil powers that came through the abuse.

I also ask, Father, that You break the spiritual union with my abuser. Grant me total spiritual freedom from _____, and I pray the blood of Jesus would cleanse my spirit as it is restored to me. I pray any door of sensual thought, action, or attraction toward _____ would be forever closed. Dear God, make me spiritually whole again.

I praise You, Father God, for loving me. You promised in Your Word that You will give a garland of beauty for ashes, the oil of joy for mourning, and a garment of praise for the spirit of heaviness (Isa. 61:3). And You told me, "If the Son shall make you free, you shall be free indeed" (John 8:36 NASB).

In the powerful name of Jesus, Amen.[11]

Our Lord is the door that offers new life for those who want to exchange their old one because of pain and sorrow. May this prayer be only the beginning of God's full and complete healing for you.

Pressing On

If you have experienced any physical consequences from the abuse, make an appointment with a caring, understanding physician to openly discuss your situation. Some possible repercussions may be a sexually transmitted disease, damage to delicate tissues, or even an unwanted pregnancy that you either ended or delivered to term. You may have to make a few calls and do some interviews over the telephone, but wait until you are comfortable with a certain doctor before you go in for a complete evaluation. An insensitive physician could set you back rather than help you.

It is also completely understandable if you have intense inner and/or outer emotional conflicts due to the molestation. If you are struggling with unresolved pain from past sexual abuse that keeps resurfacing in your marriage or in your relationships with family members or friends, find a good Christian therapist who has been specifically trained to help victims overcome the trauma of sexual abuse. It is essential to give yourself permission to make your emotional healing a priority.

If finances are an issue, remember that God promises to supply all your needs. One option is to ask if your counselor will work out a payment scale you can afford. No matter what your situation is, do whatever it takes to get the help you need. If you are unsure of who to go to in your area, you can call Focus on the Family, 1-800-A-FAMILY (232-6459), and ask for the counseling department. Although Focus does not offer long-term counseling over the phone, they do have lists of qualified counselors and their fields of expertise for most areas in the United States.

Another avenue to help further the healing process is to renew your mind by memorizing and reviewing Bible verses that encourage you. I've heard this is especially helpful if recurrent scenes of your molestation plague you when you're engaged in lovemaking with your husband. The list of verses in the section of this chapter titled "Roadblocks" can get you started. If you would like more, several verses in the Song of Songs extol the beauty of married, physical love. This is one of my favorite passages:

> ... my love's kisses flow from his lips to mine.
>
> I am my lover's.
>> I'm all he wants. I'm all the world to him!
>
> Come, dear lover—
>> let's tramp through the countryside.
>
> Let's sleep at some wayside inn,
>> then rise early and listen to bird-song.
>
> Let's look for wildflowers in bloom,
>> blackberry bushes blossoming white,
>
> Fruit trees festooned with cascading flowers.
>
> And there I'll give myself to you,
>> my love to your love!
>
> Song of Songs 7:9–12 (MSG)

Eugene Peterson's introduction to the Song of Songs in *The Message* says, "The Song is a convincing witness that men and women were created physically, emotionally and spiritually to live in love." What an excellent reminder of God's ultimate purpose and plan for married love, even though painful memories and unhealed hurts would cause us to forget.

The Journey Ends with New Beginnings

Dear friend, as our journey through the past ends, please know I empathize with you and am praying for your complete restoration. Keep in mind that even when that day comes, scars may remain. The difference between a scab and a scar is that the former is still tender and can bleed or ooze when touched. A scar reminds us we were once wounded, but it doesn't cause us intense pain anymore. Even Jesus, though He rose from the grave and went to heaven to be with His Father, still bears the scars of what each of us did to Him. When others see the scars of our pasts, we hope they will know we have suffered and therefore are able to extend compassion. Perhaps they will also know they've found a safe and trustworthy guide, a woman who's been set free and is glad to accompany them on their own journey to healing.

LIGHTEN UP!

The man and his wife were both naked, and they felt no shame.

Genesis 2:25

"Every strength has a weakness, and every weakness has a strength." I've found this to be wise counsel numerous times. If a friend is complaining her husband is miserly with their finances, I remind her he has also saved a sizable nest egg for their retirement. If a teen in our house is easily upset and lets me know exactly what he is feeling, I stop and remember it is this same teen who expresses love and caring freely to any and all who need it.

In the same way, many wonderful Christian women were raised to be upright and moral regarding their sexuality and have kept themselves pure until marriage. But the downside is that they haven't been encouraged to be enticing to their husbands. I hate to say this, but many loving, Christian wives can be boring or even prudish in the bedroom! In the area of sexual excitement, our unbelieving counterparts can have us beat—and for all the wrong reasons. They are less inhibited because they have no moral compass. They keep themselves in shape and look better physically because they don't feel Christ's acceptance of simply being loved for who they are.

Secret 6

What's a Christian woman to do? Can we be sensual and godly at the same time? Is it unchristian to wear a lacy thong and do an erotic dance for your husband in the privacy of your bedroom? Can the world's best soccer mom magically transform into her husband's wildest dream? Please understand I'm not trying to add one more thing to your already impossibly long to-do list. What I'm talking about is not something to *do*, but something to *be*. Would you be willing to rethink your entire life, prayerfully reprioritizing so the emotional, sexual, and romantic relationship with your husband gets second place only to your relationship with Jesus?

The chapters in this book are in a specific order for a reason. The first four chapters mainly address emotional issues and needs: expectations, privacy, helping one another to feel loved, and recapturing the joy in your relationship. The previous chapter took a decidedly different turn and spoke to serious spiritual matters. This chapter is about capitalizing on all we've talked about before, so that your sexual relationship with your husband is everything you'd both like it to be and more. Secret 6 is learn to lighten up in the area of physical intimacy with God's special gift to you—your husband. By the time you've read this far, I hope you're excited about reaping the benefits of a relationship that sizzles on every level.

Take a Deep Breath

Instead of bombarding you with tons of creative ideas that may or may not appeal to you and your husband (we'll get to those later), I'm starting this section with a special assignment. Create a private moment for you and your hubby, take a deep breath, and ask him, "What would be your idea of fun in our sexual relationship?" If your husband is a man of few words, you might wrap your arms around him and say, "Show me," instead of "Tell me."

I know this is a scary request! You may be uncomfortable with what he requests or fear possible rejection. Try not to give in to "what ifs." Offer any conceivable negative outcomes up to the Lord and go for it! Most husbands are delighted to answer your thought-provoking question—after they've picked themselves up off the floor!

When we are asked what *we'd* like to experience during intimacy, our inclinations usually lean toward the romantic—softly glowing candles, soothing music, sweet-smelling sheets, and no interruptions. A fresh bouquet of flowers and a night off from mom duty to soak in the tub before we retire with our husbands will turn our love monitors up from barely flickering to a blazing fire!

> Most husbands want to please us and make sure we cherish our passionate moments together as much as they do.

Men, on the other hand, often have different notions of what they'd like to experience with their wives. I asked an expert on the subject (my husband of twenty-four years) what men in general long for. He said, "The important thing to most men is knowing that their wives enjoy the sexual relationship—that she looks forward to making love and being fulfilled by him. No man likes to feel his wife doesn't want to be touched by him or that she tries to avoid physical intimacy with him." I'm not going to divulge Stu's specific requests for fun; after all, that falls under the "hedge of privacy" I talked about in chapter 4. Isn't it nice to know, however, that most husbands want to please us and make sure we cherish our passionate moments together as much as they do?

Ten Things God Forbids

What if you approach your husband in all sincerity and with the right motives to improve sexual intimacy, and he responds with a suggestion or request you don't feel you can comply with? Did you know God actually prohibits certain sexual activities even within marriage? Here is a list called "Sexual Boundaries in Marriage" taken from the book *Intimate Issues*.[1]

1. *Fornication*: From the Greek word *porneia*, it's defined as "sexual relations with anyone outside of the marriage relationship," including adultery and sex with a prostitute or a stepparent.

2. *Adultery*: This is sex with anyone other than your spouse. Adultery is a serious sin in God's eyes, even if it's mental or emotional rather than physical.

3. *Homosexuality*: This is sexual desire for or relations with someone of the same gender. The Bible is clear in its opposition to this sexual practice.

4. *Impurity and debauchery*: The New Testament often warns against impurity. Several Greek words are translated as *impurity*. To become "impure" (Greek, *molyno*) can mean to lose one's virginity or to become defiled due to living out a secular or pagan (nonbelieving) lifestyle. The word *rupos* often refers to moral uncleanness in general.

5. *Orgies*: An orgy is sexual activity with a group and is a direct violation of numbers 1, 2, and 4 above.

6. *Prostitution*: This is when a woman or man pays for or receives money for sex. It is morally wrong according to the Bible.

7. *Lustful Passions*: This does not refer to the powerful,

God-given sexual desire of a married man and woman toward one another. It is unrestrained, indiscriminate sexual desire for men or women other than one's spouse.

8. *Sodomy*: This interesting word some Christians have mistakenly equated with oral sex, but this is not the way the term was used in the Bible. The sodomites in the Bible were male homosexuals or temple prostitutes, either male or female. In the Old Testament, the word often refers to men lying with men, but it has nothing to do with the relationship between a man and his wife. The English word means male intercourse or intercourse with animals.

9. *Obscenity and coarse jokes*: The Bible clearly speaks against this in Ephesians 4:29 where Paul admonished us that no "unwholesome" word is to come out of our mouths. The Greek word literally means "rotten" or "decaying." We are also told to avoid "silly talk," which in Greek means "to

> We have to recognize the fine line between the good-natured sexual humor that can pass between a husband and wife within the privacy of their relationship and the inappropriate, public, crass jokes that are unacceptable.

turn a phrase well." We have all been around people who make sexual innuendos out of innocent phrases. This is called "coarse jesting" in the King James Version of the Bible and is not honoring to God.

We have to recognize the fine line between the good-natured sexual humor that can pass between a husband and wife within the privacy of their relationship and the inappropriate, public, crass jokes that are unacceptable. As a rule of thumb, if either of you feels convicted or uneasy with the language or humor being used between the two of you, defer to the spouse who is uncomfortable.

10. *Incest*: This is sexual relations between any close relatives, whether related by blood or marriage, and is specifically forbidden in Scripture. The entire eighteenth chapter of Leviticus explains in detail which relationships are considered incestuous.

Love Defiled

Whenever I give this special husband assignment to women's groups, two concerns always arise. The first is "I asked my husband what his idea of fun in our sexual relationship would be, and he said he wants to watch X-rated or pornographic movies together. Do I have to do this? Is this right?" Even if your gut reaction to such a request is disgust, please take your disappointment to the Lord before you interact with your husband.

My initial response to this situation is always "Has he done this before? Do you know if your husband has a problem with pornography?" If she is sure her husband is just curious and truly isn't involved with pornography, I suggest she take his hand and say, "Honey, I want our sexual relationship to be fun and exciting, just like you do. But I *know* we can have what we both want by honoring God and each other and not bringing this sort of thing into our home or our lives."

The scourge of pornography has marred and ruined countless marriages. Innocent wives beat themselves up with false guilt because they believe the misguided husband who says, "You haven't satisfied me the way you should, so what do you expect?" Deceived men toy with *Playboy* and other lewd magazines but soon move on to more explicit material via the Internet or videos. In their foolishness they forsake the true satisfaction of the marital relationship for the false gratification of a lie.

> Pornography violates almost every biblical sexual boundary. It is "a mistress, an adulteress."

Pornography violates almost every sexual boundary mentioned in the previous list. It is "a mistress, an adulteress. Her goal is to rape your husband's soul and lead him [*and your marriage*] to the grave"[2] (italics mine). You aren't required as a wife—nor should you as a Christian—to participate in any pornographic or promiscuous activity with your husband. This includes watching X-rated videos or going to topless bars. Neither are you "obligated to act out any sexual situations with your husband that are derived from a fantasy life fed by pornography."[3]

If you (yes, women also struggle with pornography) or your husband are caught in this deceitful web of sin, different avenues of support are available depending on whether you are the offender or the one offended. Check the resource list at the back of this book to help lift you and your husband out of the dark pit of pornography and restore your relationship.

The Prime Directive

It makes me laugh that God has led me to talk about making marriages sizzle. You wouldn't know it from what I write, but I am modest at heart. Some subjects are incredibly awkward for me, and I would rather just pass over them!

This being said, the second most frequently asked question regards oral sex. This is what I hear: "My husband says his idea of fun in our sexual relationship would be to have, or have more, oral sex." Again women ask me, "Do I have to do this? Is it right?" Oh, how I wish I could skip over this issue, ladies, but I just can't. It is too important to too many men, and too many Christian wives have made this a hill they would rather die on than give in to.

> Are you acting out of genuine love for one another?

What does the Bible say about oral sex? According to many experts and scholars, the Bible is essentially silent, or "veiled," on any mandates for or against oral sex.[4] Since we have no direct "rule from heaven,"[5] let's take a look at the perspective of Dr. Lewis Smedes, a professor of theology from Fuller Seminary.

> ... it is likely the only restraint [besides the biblical prohibitions mentioned previously for the sexual relationship] is the feeling of the other person. If one partner has guilt feelings about oral sex play, the Christian response will be to honor that partner until they adjust their feelings. On the other hand, if the partner has reservations rooted in some fixed ideas that sex is little more than a necessary evil anyway, they have an obligation to be taught, tenderly and lovingly, of the joys of sexual freedom in Christ.[6]

If God does not specifically prohibit something in Scripture, like oral sex, it is probably permitted. This applies as long as both the husband and wife want to participate. The prime directive is acting out of genuine love for one another.

If you have already done your special husband assignment and have asked your beloved what would make your intimate times together more fun, God bless you! I know the issue of oral sex, as well as other suggestions that take us out of our comfort zones, can make some women squeamish. If this is true of you, ask the Lord to help you determine in your heart to let go of any unscriptural restraints you have placed on yourself or your husband. At the same time, ask your husband not to force you to run ahead of your emotional readiness. The greatest contentment and satisfaction for both of you lies in mutual consent, growing together emotionally and physically.

> The greatest contentment and satisfaction for both of you lies in mutual consent, growing together emotionally and physically.

Patty and James have an intensely passionate marriage. Their highs are sky high, while their lows can dip down to the bottom of the barrel. During one of those depressing lows, they attended a couples' Bible study. The instruction for the night was, "Tell the group one thing you appreciate about your spouse." Patty thought and thought, but couldn't come up with anything at the moment. When it was her turn to speak, she looked down at her hands, which were clenched in her lap, and said, "James is wonderful in bed. He's great! A generous lover."

After a stunned silence, loud laughter and shouts of "Way to go, James!" rang through the room. James walked on air the next couple of weeks, and their discouraging low immediately sky-rocketed in the other direction.

How bold Patty was to praise her husband in this sensitive area in mixed company! I wanted to find out how she came to adore her husband's lovemaking skills. Her answer surprised me.

"For years James and I had an okay sexual relationship. Every once in a while he'd suggest new ideas for us, but I always resisted. I just wasn't comfortable and didn't feel like I had to adjust to his requests. The neat thing is, the longer we were married, the more loved, safe, and at ease I felt with him, even with all of our ups and downs. Little by little I began following James's lead in our sexual relationship. He's a creative man, and the physical oneness and intimacy we share now far surpasses anything we experienced in the early years of our marriage."

> As the husband loves, adores, and connects with his wife, his affirmation ignites her passion.

What Women Want

For the most part, women are responders, aren't we? Drs. Cliff and Joyce Penner wrote, "A man has the key to a woman's sexuality: affirmation. As the husband loves, adores, and connects with his wife, his affirmation ignites her passion. She is then open to invite her husband sexually, and her invitation validates him."[7]

Perhaps your husband already knows this about you and

makes every effort to stoke your romantic fires. If so, thank the Lord for such a sensitive guy. Most husbands would love for their wives to be more spontaneous and uninhibited in the bedroom. The problem is many men aren't tuned in to why their wives aren't as excited about physical intimacy as they are.

This book is aimed at you because women are usually the ones who care

> We are more likely to respond to our husbands based on how they treat us rather than to jump ahead and set the pace.

about improving the quality of a relationship. But the truth is we are more likely to respond to our husbands based on how they treat us rather than to jump ahead and set the pace. In all my years of ministering to women, I have never heard complaints from a wife whose husband is acting as the loving, gentle leader God wants him be. I know some women are the major source of problems in a relationship, but most wives I talk with desperately want to elevate the level of intimacy and passion in their marriage, yet they feel unable to make it happen. Their husbands are either unable or unwilling to change. If more men understood that most of us would gladly follow a faithful, compassionate leader, I'm sure they'd be amazed at how much sizzle would result.

Since every marriage is unique, and each of us has different wants and needs, the key to generating a positive response from you may not look the same as it would for someone else. However, you have access to a relationship tool that has helped thousands of couples draw closer to one another emotionally and physically. It should leave both you and your husband feeling completely satisfied. That tool is called "relationship meetings."

Meetings for Her

Kent Miller, a licensed marriage and family counselor, often uses the following illustration to explain why scheduling specific times to discuss your relationship or to have sex is beneficial for many couples. He says,

> If a person is starving and doesn't know where her next meal is coming from, she will eat whenever food is available. Not only that, when she isn't eating, she is constantly thinking about when she will get to eat again. Where will she find the food she needs? What will she do if she doesn't get to eat when she wants or needs to? In other words, the starving individual becomes obsessed with food. It's the same for a man or woman who is starving emotionally or sexually in a marriage.
>
> When a husband feels starved sexually, he will frequently demand sex from his wife. He isn't really concerned about her; instead it becomes all about making sure he will get his physical needs met. In the same way, when a wife feels starved emotionally because her husband doesn't listen to her or take her concerns seriously, she will complain, nag, and constantly bring up problems because she never knows when or if he will really listen to her and care about what's bothering her.

Kent's solution to these valid longings is "relationship meetings." These meetings have one of two angles: emotional or sexual. Ideally your husband is supposed to initiate emotional meetings, especially if you aren't feeling loved or listened to. The purpose of these meetings is to discuss any negatives about your relationship, issues with kids, finances, whatever is causing stress in your marriage. Your husband begins by asking, "How do you feel about our relationship?" You get to share everything that is on your heart, and he is not allowed to interrupt or correct. He just listens and gives feedback such as, "I see; so what you're saying is ..." Then, it's his turn. After you have both covered your relationship, you are free to move on to any other tensions that need to be discussed. The goal isn't to solve all your problems in one sitting, but rather to limit the amount of time a couple focuses on the difficulties that are interfering with their love for one another.

The meeting parameters are that you must meet at least two times a week but not more than three. Each meeting is to be no shorter than twenty minutes and no longer than an hour. In addition, allow at least one day between meetings but not more than three. This gives you and your spouse some breathing room in case there is tension around your home. Furthermore, you're not allowed emotional meetings on dates unless you and your husband are getting along and the exchange is completely positive. Outside the meetings, neither of you is allowed to bring up anything negative, critical, demeaning, or hurtful—unless, of course, it's a true emergency.

The reason these meetings are important is because they work! Even reluctant husbands are quickly won over when they realize they can call home or walk through the door and not be bombarded with their wives' latest upset. And a wife relaxes, knowing she will get the opportunity to talk about all that's troubling her to a captive audience of one, her husband, at their next relationship meeting.

Kevin and Nicole had new life breathed into their marriage through relationship meetings. Blessed with three adopted children, they struggle daily because two of their children have bipolar disorder. Nicole confided in me that her marriage had completely deteriorated due to the constant upheaval in their home.

"Every time Kevin and I talk, it's to vent about the latest upset with one of the kids. I hate it!" she said. "We've given up going on dates because all we do is rehash what's wrong in our lives."

I told Nicole about emotional meetings and asked if Kevin would be open to trying them. Fortunate wife that she is, she answered, "Oh, he'll do whatever I suggest. He's always up for things that keep our relationship strong."

Just one week later, Nicole reported, "Denise, you saved my marriage!"

I started laughing and asked, "How so?"

"Those relationship meetings. Kevin and I agreed to try them for one week. Saturday night I'd had a really hard day with the kids, but nothing out of the ordinary for our house. Kevin was leaving for a reunion with some flight instructors he'd been looking forward to for months. As he left, I was so tempted to whine and complain. I knew if I did, he'd stay home with me. But we'd had a meeting the night before, so instead of bringing up the troubles of that day, I just swallowed hard and said, 'Have a good time, honey!'

"He paused, looked at me, and said, 'Are you sure?' I put on my best cheerful face and replied, 'Absolutely.' When he arrived home later that night, he said, 'Nicole, I had the best time. I was a little worried about leaving you with the kids, though. Did you do okay?' I gave Kevin a hug and told him, 'I'll let you know at our next meeting.'"

Nicole went on to say, "I never realized what a bad attitude I had until I had to wait for our relationship meetings to download. For the first time in months, Kevin and I actually feel hopeful about our marriage, even if things continue to be difficult with the kids."

By curbing the amount of time spent dwelling on what's hard in life, we're forced to live out Philippians 4:8 (MSG): "Summing it all up, friends, I'd say you'll do best by filling your minds and meditating on things true, noble, reputable, authentic, compelling, gracious—the best, not the worst; the beautiful, not the ugly; things to praise, not things to curse." God's Word is always true. You will lighten up, the atmosphere in your home will feel better, and your marriage won't be such a drag when you raise the negatives only at your meetings.

Meetings for Him

Many husbands, when they learn about emotional meetings, have a knee-jerk reaction. "Well, that's fine for my wife, but what about me?" Reassure your man that good things are in store for him, too. One of the simplest ways to ensure meetings happen for both partners is to link your emotional meetings to your sexual relationship. If the frequency of your sexual interludes is an issue for your husband, tell him you will gladly have a love-

> When a woman feels emotionally close to her husband, she will often embrace physical intimacy much more readily.

making session for every emotional meeting he provides. When a woman feels emotionally close to her husband, she will often embrace physical intimacy much more readily.

I know planned meetings sound unromantic and overly rigid. But the reality is, most men are thrilled to know they can count on a warm and willing wife two to three times a week, and most wives are delighted to know they get to emotionally connect with their husbands on a regular basis. The happy ending is a woman who feels loved and heard and therefore "lightens up" emotionally and physically and a husband who reaps the rewards of a joyful, contented wife as well as renewed passion in their sexual relationship.

Even marriages that aren't struggling benefit from this arrangement because it's always a treat to affirm one another, to be intentional about telling our spouses we love them. If things are going well, you and your husband get to spend at least twenty minutes focusing on what's great in your relationship, what you appreciate about each other, and maybe your hopes and dreams for your future. A good way to start is to ask each other, "What was the best part of your day?" and then to tell one another, "The thing I appreciated most about you today (or yesterday, last week, and so forth) is _____." Emotional meetings aren't only for hurting couples, but they seem to be more essential during difficult times.

Of course, there are always exceptions to the rules. Some men feel emotionally disconnected from their wives, and some women hunger for their husbands' touch. I pray you will take what's helpful and adapt whichever principles are needed so you can enjoy your marriage to the fullest.

Beauty and the Bride

Even if everything is wonderful, many women still feel inhibited about their bodies and therefore find it difficult to lighten up in their sexual relationship with their husbands. I've met beautifully proportioned women who obsessively focus on the extra five pounds they're carrying around rather than allowing their husband to enjoy their beauty. On the other hand, I know average women, puckered thighs and all, who are altogether comfortable with their bodies and aren't ashamed to parade around seductively in front of their husbands.

Men are visual, so even a glimpse of you getting undressed and ready for bed can be enough to get your husband in the mood. It's hard to flaunt what you've got, however, if you don't like the package God's given you. Stop for a minute and think— what makes you feel sexy? Is it a particular hairstyle or when you've hit your ideal weight? Do you feel sexy only when certain body parts are covered up or when all the lights are turned off? (How much fun is *that* when you can't even see each other!)

Maybe you used to like your body, but after babies or surgeries or simply old age, you'd rather throw a flannel nightgown over your head than reveal what's underneath. It's true we have no control over what pregnancy, illness, and aging do to our bodies. But unfortunately, some women have just plain given up and let themselves go. An attitude like that develops from a myriad of reasons, yet the Bible reminds us that our bodies are the temple of the Holy Spirit. God Himself dwells within us! What an awesome responsibility. How can we get ourselves back on track without becoming obsessed if we've neglected the gift of life and health God has given us?

> One of the best ways to jump-start your motivation is to get out your wedding pictures and look at yourself as a bride.

One of the best ways to jump-start your motivation is to get out your wedding pictures and look at yourself as a bride. Then take a look in the nearest mirror. How closely do you resemble the beauty you were when you got married? Every time I suggest this to an audience, the room erupts with moans and giggles. But your husband married you because he was attracted to *you*, to the exact kind of woman that you are.

Some men like the natural look: little or no makeup, an easy-to-care-for hairstyle, and Eddie Bauer hiking clothes. Other men go for a more refined appearance: nicely coiffed hair, expertly applied makeup, polished nails, and the latest outfit from Nordstrom. Many of us fall somewhere in between these two styles or even go back and forth. (I always tell people if it wasn't for makeup and hot curlers, I don't think Stu would have noticed me!)

Along these same lines, you need to accept the body type you have. Some women are muscular, lean, and athletic. Others are round and curvy like Marilyn Monroe. One type isn't better than the other; they're just different. Your basic shape was determined in your genes from the moment of your conception. One of the healthiest things you can do for yourself—and your husband—is to thank the Lord for the way He made you, and then make the most of it. If you're thin and small breasted, don't you think your husband realized this before you were married? It's something everyone can tell, even when you have all your clothes on. The same is true if you're more like the Renaissance models the famous artist Rubens painted, full figured and voluptuous. Again, most of us fall somewhere in the middle. I would venture to say few of us match the fake, air-brushed, surgically corrected perfection of media models. And, if we're honest, neither do our husbands. An enthusiastic, uninhibited attitude matters a thousand times more than a flawless body.

> One of the healthiest things you can do for yourself—and your husband—is to thank the Lord for the way He made you, and then make the most of it.

Reality Check

Just because we're married and reasonably secure that our husbands won't leave us over a superficial aspect like our appearance, we're still responsible to take care of ourselves. The overarching concern should be your health. Many great books and resources are available to get you healthy and keep you there, but here are some general reminders.

Are you at a weight appropriate for your height? The old standard was one hundred pounds for a woman five feet tall, adding five pounds for every inch after that. Today's charts are more generous and take into account your bone structure and age. The best rule of thumb is to stay within ten pounds—either over or under—your correct weight. Most people know the medical risks of being overweight, but did you know it can be just as dangerous to be underweight? Your body is more prone to infections, immune system disorders, and the cessation of your menstrual cycle. Not eating too much or too little and eating the right foods will take care of most women's weight issues.

> An enthusiastic, uninhibited attitude matters a thousand times more than a flawless body.

If you need emotional support, have a metabolic disorder, or are aware of other barriers that impact your ability to gain or lose weight, make a commitment to take care of whatever isn't working and learn to treasure the body God has given you. This side of heaven, it's the only one we'll get.

You've heard this next piece of advice a million times: You should exercise several times a week. Exercise can take many different forms. It's not just working out in the gym that counts. You can walk on your lunch hour or pull weeds in the garden. Washing windows, scrubbing floors, or riding a bicycle all can keep you in good shape. Whatever activities you choose to do, remember to pick something that keeps you moving. Studies have shown exercising for only ten minutes a couple times a day raises your metabolism and helps your body burn calories more efficiently. For busy wives and moms, exercise is often the last thing on our minds. But even a little bit is better than nothing and will lift your spirits throughout the day.

> The comforting truth is that it really doesn't matter to most husbands if their wives match the image of some Hollywood movie star.

The comforting truth is that it really doesn't matter to most husbands if their wives match the image of some Hollywood movie star. What's important to them is a wife who gladly and unashamedly shares her body, heart, and soul with the man she loves. Eating well and exercising regularly are the two fundamentals available to every woman who wants to feel good and look better. Remember, no amount of makeup can imitate the glow of good health.

Many women, however, do not feel emotionally safe putting their bodies on display for their husbands. Any of the topics we've covered earlier can make you want to hide: sexual abuse, pornography, poor health, or unresolved emotional issues. If your husband has made unkind comments about your body, you have another painful hurdle to overcome.

Ladies, if any of these conditions exist in your marriage, please do whatever is in your power to right what's wrong. Don't passively accept deeply rooted problems in your relationship. Pray, get outside help, set boundaries, and pursue physical and/or emotional healing. Our goal isn't to have a perfect, flawless marriage. There's no such thing! We do, however, want to live in the healthiest marriage possible, given the two distinct personalities that are intertwined together.

Too Much of a Good Thing

A study involving men and women aged forty-five to fifty-five years old was conducted over a ten-year period. The findings revealed that those who had sexual intercourse 50 percent more often than their peers looked up to twelve years younger. Psychologist David Weeks speculated "lovemaking boosts hormones which reduce fatty tissue and increase lean muscle, giving a more youthful appearance."[8] If you've read this far and still aren't sure you want to make your marriage sizzle, wouldn't you rather have more physical intimacy with your husband than Botox injections?

As loving wives, we care about our men's health too. Noted cardiologist Dr. Mehmet Oz stated that for men to have optimum cardiac health, they should "walk, avoid fast foods, drink red wine and have regular sex, lasting about half an hour, four times a week."[9] One enthusiastic wife read these recommendations to her stressed-out husband and said, "Okay, darling. Let's give Dr. Oz's suggestions a try. You've been working hard, and I don't want you to have a heart attack." Her husband excitedly agreed, but on day five, during session three of the doctor's prescription, he said, "Does it really have to last a half hour?" And by day seven he told his wife, "Does it count if I just *think* about sex?" He'd had too much of a good thing!

How often you make love is a personal decision. What is right or normal for one marriage may not apply to another. Many experts agree that the average man needs a sexual release every three days due to the way his body is designed. For some relationships, this would be way too much. You know your husband and he knows you, so together I hope you can reach an agreement that blesses both of you. Remember the discussion on "mercy sex" from chapter 2? Not every sexual encounter has to be a gourmet feast for intimacy to take place. Sometimes short and sweet can be just as special.

Another way to get on the same page as your husband sexually is to pay attention to your body's cycles. You will usually have two weeks out of the month when you feel more energized. When your estrogen levels are high at the onset of your period and up to fourteen days afterward, you will be at your emotional and physical peak. Your body's next phase is when you ovulate. A woman's sexual desire is at its highest during this two- to three-day period. This is a perfect picture of God's wisdom to keep the human race going. By day seventeen or eighteen, your estrogen levels drop, and your body is getting ready to menstruate. For many women (and men) these are the horror days of PMS. (As one husband said, "PMS stands for 'Pack My Suitcase'!") You may be tired, grouchy, confused, and even sore. Breast tenderness is common before your period. Whatever your symptoms, it's doubtful you want to be touched.

A wise woman knows her good weeks and bad weeks. She takes advantage of her good weeks by initiating sex with her husband, being available when he is in the mood, and putting that extra energy into keeping their love life passionate. Then, on her down weeks, her husband won't feel so rejected, and she won't feel like she's depriving him.

Body cycles also include figuring out whether you and your husband are on the same sleep schedule. Does one of you get up with the sun as the other is just heading for bed? Most couples are a mix. When this is true, it can get tricky trying to find just the right time when you both have energy and are awake. One solution is to take turns accommodating each other's best time of day—then sneak in an afternoon, when you are both perky, as often as possible.

Another factor to take into account is that men and women reach their sexual peaks at different stages in life. Just when she is gearing up and enjoying the benefits of a healthy sex life, he might be winding down. Couples who have been successfully married for a number of years have learned they can adapt to almost anything—different body clocks, fluctuating hormones, even the ebb and flow of physical desire—when they really want to.

Creative Memories

In the process of writing this book, I asked many friends and acquaintances if they'd be willing to share their personal secrets for making their marriages sizzle. The common thread running throughout the following ideas is elevating the sexual relationship from just a quick, physical encounter to a higher plane, where memories are made and marriages are strengthened. As you read, I'm sure you'll agree I know some incredibly creative and romantic women. But don't think for a second that this creativity can't be a part of your life.

It's the little things in life that can mean the most to us. With this in mind, Paula has a special perfume she wears only when she and Brad are making love. It's her "signature scent," and he is the only one who ever experiences it. She also suggests not putting your lipstick on before you leave the house, so you can kiss your hubby longer.

Yvette and her husband have a certain CD they listen to only when they are intimate. She says it helps her relax and puts her in the mood, enabling her to unwind and forget about the ever-present pressures of life.

Danielle sprays their sheets with a delicious fragrance while Steve is getting ready for work in the mornings. This nonverbal signal helps him spend the day anticipating a wonderful evening together. One of my more uninhibited girlfriends asks her husband which colored thong he'd like to see her in that night—or models it for him in their bedroom that morning to get him thinking ahead. Keep in mind that this last suggestion works only if your husband has a supertight schedule or lots of self-control. Be prepared for a "morning session" if you are spontaneous enough to try this!

Another friend of mine surprised her husband at his office. Becky wore a coat and brought a picnic basket filled with yummy things to eat. Tom was glad to see her but pretty nonchalant—until she laid out a blanket and took her coat off. All she had on was some lacy undergarments. "Becky," he exclaimed, "aren't you afraid someone's going to walk in on us?" "Not really," she replied. "That's why I did this on a Saturday!" She said it didn't go quite as well as she had planned because Tom was so nervous the entire time. He did, however, appreciate his wife's thoughtfulness in conveying love to him during a stressful time in his life.

Kendra was so absorbed with their three preschoolers that she didn't realize how neglected Wayne was feeling until he turned to her one night after she flopped into bed without even a goodnight kiss and told her, "Honey, I feel like I've lost my wife! I miss you." Those few words spurred Kendra into action. The next day she drove to the local hardware store and purchased two gallons of plum-colored paint. "Purple is the color of royalty and passion," Kendra told me.

The following week when Wayne was out of town on a quick business trip, Kendra covered all the furniture in their bedroom and painted up a storm. Silk sheets and a new, matching comforter completed her love project. She said, "Working on our bedroom while Wayne was away made me miss him so much and long for him to come home. I was focused on him and our relationship in a much more powerful way than if I'd only concentrated on the kids while he was gone."

Wayne returned home to a redecorated haven and a recommitted wife. Another note here: Kendra has consistently made her husband a priority, in spite of the fact that two of their children are handicapped. She could easily bog down due to the overwhelming demands of her life. But long ago she made the choice to lighten up emotionally and physically. Kendra chose to stay close to her husband, keep her playful spirit, and not dwell on the hardships of her life. Their long-term marriage sizzles to this day, and they've been together since they were fourteen years old.

LOYALTY FOR A LIFETIME

Love is as strong as death.

Song of Songs 8:6

Today, as I begin writing this chapter on loyalty to your spouse for a lifetime, Stu and I are celebrating our twenty-fourth anniversary. Twenty-four years ago today, I was awakened with a phone call from my husband-to-be. *How sweet,* I thought. *He's calling to tell me how glad he is we're getting married today, how much he loves me, or something romantic like that.* Instead I heard, "Denise, we have to go to the hospital. My grandmother is in congestive heart failure and isn't expected to make it through the day." This was the same dear grandmother who had given Stu her engagement ring to give to me.

I remembered the superstition that the groom isn't supposed to see the bride before the wedding. But I quickly dismissed it. "That's just an old wives' tale. I'm not going to pay attention to my misgivings. I'm a Christian now; those things don't matter anymore."

We're thankful that Stu's grandmother didn't die that day. She went on to live another four years and saw the birth of two great-grandchildren. However, as the marriage I anticipated didn't always materialize and the stresses and strains came and went with each passing year, I sometimes thought back to our wedding day and wondered if we hadn't violated some secret code by seeing each other. Did Grandma Coyle's going into intensive care that morning foreshadow the wild ups and downs we've experienced throughout our marriage?

Secret 7

Loyalty for a lifetime is found in remembering your vows, whether they were traditional vows read from the Psalter or creatively written vows designed just for you and your new lover.

On one level, in my mind and my spirit, I know this isn't true. But on another level, the one that encompasses my heart and emotions, I've been puzzled at times over the amount of sheer work and determination it's taken to see secret seven—loyalty for a lifetime—cultivated in our relationship. That's why the verse at the beginning of this chapter means so much to me. True love *is* as strong as death. It isn't a flimsy, whimsical attraction that evaporates at the first sign of trouble. Oh, I know it often *feels* like that, but the truth is,

> Love is very patient and kind, never jealous or envious, never boastful or proud, never haughty or selfish or rude. Love does not demand its own way. It is not irritable or touchy. It does not hold grudges and will hardly even notice when others do it wrong. It is never glad about injustice, but rejoices whenever truth wins out. If you love someone you will be loyal to him no matter

what the cost. You will always believe in him, always
expect the best of him, and always stand your ground in
defending him.... There are three things that remain—
faith, hope and love—and the greatest of these is love. (1
Cor. 13:4–7, 13 TLB)

Many couples use this beautiful description of real love in
their wedding ceremony as a reminder that when the euphoric
head-over-heels feelings end, they can be replaced with a deeper
more other-centered emotion. This kind of love actually generates an even stronger sense of passion and excitement than that
first rush of hormones many of us encountered when we met
our spouses.

Do you remember the words you spoke before God, your
husband, and those gathered at your wedding ceremony?

Loyalty for a lifetime is found in remembering your vows,
whether they were traditional vows read from the Psalter or creatively written vows designed just for you and your new lover.

Let's close with some lasting truths that will
strengthen your relation-
ship and help keep the fires
of emotional intimacy and
passion sizzling in your
marriage.

I Take Thee

When the rough waters of
life threaten to sink your
"relation-ship," your mar-

> Think about why you
> married the man you
> did and how you felt
> about him—before
> problems began or
> stagnation set in.

riage can feel like a tiny, fragile dinghy adrift in the windswept
Atlantic. At times like this, it's helpful to recall the feelings you
had for your husband when you first met. What drew you to
him in the first place? Was it his sense of humor? The way he

treated his mother? His love for God? His strong work ethic? Think about why you married the man you did and how you felt about him—before problems began or stagnation set in.

Unless you had an arranged marriage, you chose your husband and were happy to do so! Very few of us felt forced into saying I do. But it's easy to forget the attraction you once had for each other when the pressures of life swamp your love boat. When this happens, let the powerful effect of pleasurable memories pull you in the right direction. Look at your wedding album together, reminisce on your dating days, reread old love letters. Do whatever it takes to help reignite your feelings for each other—and not just on your anniversary. Remember, you said yes to your husband over all the other men you knew.

> Do whatever it takes to help reignite your feelings for each other—and not just on your anniversary.

If you got married under less-than-ideal circumstances, you can't go back and change them now, even if you wish you could. But please don't let a less-than-perfect start define the rest of your relationship. Even if you felt unsure if marrying this guy was the right thing, it is now. Maybe you wouldn't have married the man you did—but you were pregnant and felt you should marry your baby's father. Or perhaps you had sex with your boyfriend and felt you had to marry him because you'd already been physically intimate. These legitimate issues need to be addressed. When you do, you'll often find the need for forgiveness is at the heart of our dismay.

Begin by asking God's forgiveness. Then ask one another's forgiveness, and finally, forgive yourself, which is often the hardest part for most of us. Praise God, He is more than willing to help us move beyond whatever situations clouded our dream wedding. He wants to wipe the slate clean and give our relationship a brand-new start.

Some couples choose to renew their vows either privately or before a few close friends and family in honor of their newfound devotion to each other. It's wonderful to see God create beauty from ashes, as He promises to do in Isaiah 61:3, in the lives of His children.

My Lawfully Wedded Husband

Elisabeth Elliot wrote in *Let Me Be a Woman,* a book of letters she wrote to her engaged daughter,

> You marry a man, not a woman ... but some women expect their husbands to be women, to act like women. They want marriage, with all the benefits it offers—a home, children, security, and social status, but not necessarily a man. You see, a man is likely to be bigger and louder and tougher and hungrier and dirtier than a woman expects. ... she learns that what makes her cry may make him laugh. Anything he does which seems to her unexplainable, she dismisses with [the comment] "Just like a man" as though it were a condemnation. It is a man she married after all and she is lucky if he acts like a man.[1]

Ladies, have you ever wished your husband acted more like your ... *girlfriend?* I confess I have at times. When I've just poured my heart out to Stu and I get a one-syllable grunt (which I've learned means he either agrees with me or doesn't know what to say); when hair from his beard is all over the bathroom counters and not just in the sink; when it's a gorgeous Sunday afternoon, and he'd rather stay inside watching the Denver Broncos play football—then I long for him to be more like one of the girls!

In today's culture, men and their preferences are often looked on with disdain. The masculine characteristics that set them apart from women are somehow depicted as bad, something to be squelched. For instance, don't let your little boys play with guns or they may turn into serial killers. I tried that with our oldest, Luke, and do you know what he did? He ate his bread into the shape of a gun!

A none-too-subtle message is sent to our husbands and sons that only *women* have the personality traits all people should have. No matter how much your husband may frustrate you in typical male ways, this kind of thinking is dead wrong. God created both male and female and called them good. Not just women and not just men. So the next time your husband irritates you with his lack of sensitivity, his cavalier attitude toward the laundry hamper, or his insatiable need to go hunting or fishing, thank God that you were attracted to a man, that you chose to marry a man, and that in His wisdom, God made men in the first place. Then go vent to a close girlfriend about the latest "man thing" he did that bugged you.

Another aspect of being married to a man is understanding the unique pressures men face. Since men are wired to focus on one thing at a time, to go out and conquer, his work can often feel like the "other woman" in a marriage. I have a friend whose attitude toward her husband is a quiet rebuke to me. Carly's husband, Phil, has always done very physical work. He builds and remodels houses. Carly devotes a lot of time to maintaining their home, cooking from scratch, sewing, and taking wonderful care of their three children—besides holding down two part-time jobs.

Even with her workload, however, Carly is always so sensitive to Phil's—or to any man's—exhaustion due to work. Instead of comparing her schedule to Phil's, she is always quick to comment, "Oh, Phil's worked so hard this week; he really needs a break." Stu really appreciates Carly because she often makes comments like "I bet Stu's tired; he works so hard." It's a little embarrassing because I tend to forget how hard Stu works. I guess I assume he's used to it by now!

Since you married a man, come to terms with the fact that you might have to remind him once in a while when you need some romance. Every woman longs for her beloved to intuitively

> Come to terms with the fact that you might have to remind him once in a while when you need some romance.

know when she wants to be swept off her feet and cherished. And sometimes our guys come through. Those are special days, aren't they? More often than not, however, you may need to remind your husband that you need romance. If he's feeling good about your relationship, he thinks you are too, and that all is fine and dandy in the hearts and flowers department. I'll admit it takes a little bit of the shine off, knowing we have to bring it to their attention. But isn't that better than seething inside because he hasn't been romantic since your anniversary nine months ago? The choice is yours. Just keep in mind your husband may not realize why you're wilting, and a gentle prompt from you may be all he needs to start the romance engine.

Finally, if you aren't legally married to the man you are emotionally and sexually involved with, I pray you will take seriously God's instructions to make your union holy and lasting in the eyes of God and the people you love. God designed the institution of marriage for the woman's emotional security as well as her physical and sexual protection.

Here are some biblical principles and references that explain this view:

Marriage is God's idea (Gen. 2:18–24).

Marriage is the best environment for raising children (Mal. 2:14–15).

Marriage is permanent (Matt. 19:6).

Marriage is based on the practice of love, not feelings (Eph. 5:21–33).

Marriage is a living symbol of Christ and the church (Eph. 5:23, 32).

Marriage is good and honorable (Heb. 13:4).

You will never know how many blessings you are forfeiting by forgoing marriage. It is more than just a ceremony or a piece of paper, as so many are fond of claiming. It is a solemn covenant, taken for life and honored by God, for those who choose to do so.

To Love

One of my best friends used to ask her husband, "Why did you marry me?" She longed to hear, "Because you're beautiful. Because you're wonderful. Because there was no one else in the world for me but you." Instead what she heard time after time was, "Because I chose to." At first, Robin was crushed. "You're not very romantic," she often replied. But as the years went by, she understood Carl's motives. He was telling her that his love was unconditional, unchanging. Carl was offering her *agape* love, the sacrificial love for others not based on actions or feelings, but grounded in his commitment to God and to her.

Robin told me, "I know 'I chose to marry you' doesn't sound romantic, but it's exactly what every woman's heart desires, whether she knows it or not, because it's permanent and lasting. I'm secure in Carl's love for me. I never have to doubt or wonder if he loves me, because his love doesn't come and go, depending on his latest mood or how I perform as a wife and mother."

In this changing, insecure, unstable world, the promise of committed love, no matter what the circumstances, is an inestimable treasure most of us would give anything for. You may have spoken the words at your wedding, but do you try to live out this type of love in your relationship on a daily basis?

> Don't look at someone else's marriage and assume what's working for them will automatically work for you and your husband.

Here's a simple assignment I like to give women: Ask your husband each morning, "Is there anything you want me to do for you today?" Even if his love language isn't service, it will show him he is a priority in your life and that you want to be a helpmate to him. Another good question that is more involved and will require some thought is "Tell me the one thing that is important to you for me to concentrate on or accomplish to show my love for you." Because every husband is different and every marriage has its own personality, your beloved's answer will reflect a longing or need particular to his life and no one else's. Don't look at someone else's marriage and assume what's working for them will automatically work for you and your husband. Take the politically correct bumper sticker "Celebrate Diversity" and apply it to your relationship.

Honor and Cherish

Honor and cherish sound like old-fashioned words that aren't part of our daily vocabulary anymore. *Honor* brings to mind knights in shining armor and dueling to the death to defend one's reputation; *cherish* conjures up going to extreme measures to make sure a woman feels taken care of. But what do these words, which we probably said at our own weddings, really mean? *Webster's* defines *honor* as "to show great respect or high regard for; to treat with deference and courtesy,"[2] while *cherish* means "to hold dear, feel or show love for; to take good care of, foster or protect."[3] Even though these words aren't as common today, if we actively tried to live them out, our marriages would grow stronger.

> *Honor, cherish.* Even though these words aren't as common today, if we actively tried to live them out, our marriages would grow stronger.

What does an atmosphere of respect, deference, and courtesy—honor—look like in the home? Here are several factors:

1. Not interrupting when someone else is talking
2. Using the "magic" words: please, thank you, and you're welcome
3. Placing equal value on opinions that are different from yours
4. Allowing for different tastes and preferences
5. Not ridiculing one another with sarcasm or hurtful jokes

A wife also shows honor to her husband by placing their relationship above her relationship with parents, sisters, children, or friends. Ask yourself if you spend more time with your girlfriends or work or hobbies than with your spouse. Would you say your husband is your best friend? Are you his? Many men are so busy with work and other obligations that we wives are often their primary source of friendship. Even if they interact with other men through work or sports, they often feel lonely because they aren't connecting on more than a superficial level.

> One way we show our beloved honor is by affirming his dreams, desires, and aspirations.

One way we show our beloved honor is by affirming his dreams, desires, and aspirations. If you're married to a "dreamer" this may be hard, because you've heard so many plans and seen only a few come to fruition. But the alternative is a man who quits talking, which is one of the biggest complaints I hear from women. Being married to a dreamer myself, I've learned I don't need to get overly concerned or panicked when Stu is dreaming out loud—until he begins to act on what he's shared.

Honor also involves giving our men the respect they crave. The average husband would rather hear "Honey, have I told you lately three things I respect about you?" than "Darling, I love you because ..." Try it with your guy and see. The wife of a fairly uncommunicative husband popped her head into his office and said, "You know, I've been meaning to tell you some things I really respect about you." Then she left the room. He tracked her down on the other side of house and asked, "So, are you going to tell me those things you respect?" She did, and it meant so much to him that he opened up to her for the next half hour about what was on his heart.

If honor is love expressed nobly through self-control and

respect, cherish is the softer side of love. As women, we long to feel cherished—protected, taken care of, looked out for, treated with sweet consideration. In return, many husbands feel cherished when we do "womanly" things for them. The times we make them a special meal, rub their feet, bring them a cup of coffee when they're working, don't overbook their social schedule, rent their favorite movie, or serve steak instead of vegetable quiche.

> Many husbands feel cherished when we do "womanly" things for them.

My son recently told me he didn't think he could date a young woman he was mildly interested in because, as he got to know her, he realized he needed—in his words—more of a "girly girl." He said it never occurred to this young lady to offer to make him a sandwich or get him a hot drink after he'd been working out in the cold all day. In fact, once when he asked her politely if she wouldn't mind getting him something, she said, "Get it yourself!"

When you're done laughing, as I secretly did, and you understand this girl was on break from school and doesn't work, you'll get what my son meant. One way a woman can express her love to her man is through all the little things she does to smooth his way and make him feel taken care of.

For Better, For Worse

Ask anybody. We would rather be married in "for better" times than "for worse." For better is when everyone is healthy, your bank account is padded, your parents love being grandparents, you're content with your home, you both have enjoyable work, and your days are spent in pleasant compatibility. Some years you may feel blessed to get even five days like that! For better times are precious gifts from God we should never take for granted. But many of us have an underlying attitude problem, expecting life to give us this lifestyle all the time.

If you want more of these better times in your marriage, you may have to let go of some unhealthy idealism. It's not wrong to have hopes and desires for your marriage, but accepting what is instead of always longing for what you don't have will bring you the most peace. For instance, some couples have great compatibility but not a lot of passion. Other couples have tons of passion but aren't very compatible. A fortunate few possess both, but if that doesn't describe your marriage, ask God how to make the most of what you have, given your and your husband's personalities and temperaments.

> If you want more of these better times in your marriage, you may have to let go of some unhealthy idealism.

Another key to contentment is to keep your envy in check. Despite how perfect the neighbor's relationship appears to be, every family has its own difficulties and quirks. If you truly knew a certain situation, you probably wouldn't want to trade. If the family or marriage you envy isn't hiding any secrets, and the love and happiness they share is for real, prayerfully consider whether what's working for them might be beneficial in your own household.

And during those "for worse" times, please don't let the *D* word—divorce—be an option. Be careful not to hastily file for divorce just because you're presently in pain. Our generation has decided personal happiness is the god we will serve, and almost

Mutual forgiveness, humility toward God and one another, and prayer can be the greatest factors in keeping couples together during the "for worse" times.

every decision we make is passed through that filter. Drs. Henry Cloud and John Townsend agree: "People who always want to be happy and pursue it above all else are some of the most miserable people in the world.... Happiness is a result of doing the character work we need so that we are content and joyful in whatever circumstances we find ourselves.... If happiness is our guide and it goes away, we assume something is wrong."[4] Mutual forgiveness, humility toward God and one another, and prayer can be the greatest factors in keeping couples together during the for worse times.

For Richer, For Poorer

Just like "for better," if given the choice we'd all rather be rich, right? When you can't make ends meet without cutting out necessities, or when there's never any extra floating around, stress levels run high. On the other hand, having more than enough can sometimes feel empty. How many couples, once they achieve their financial goals, drift apart? How many times do people turn into misers or workaholics because they are driven by financial insecurity? Proverbs 30:8–9 (TLB) gives us good guidelines to pray for: "Give me neither poverty nor riches! Give me just enough to satisfy my needs! For if I grow rich, I may become content without God. And if I am too poor, I may steal, and thus insult God's holy name."

When you and your husband are working to the best of your abilities, and it still doesn't seem like there's enough money to go around, check your attitude by asking yourself these questions:

1. *Are we doing our best to provide for the family, given the gifts and talents God has given us?* Not everyone is wired for college. Not everyone has the business savvy to run a corporation well. Look objectively at both yourself and the man you married, and if you know in your heart you are both hitting the mark, accept whatever financial limits or abundance go along with the package.

2. *Can we do anything to improve our financial situation?* Could you take on a job without sacrificing the welfare of your family? Another option many stay-at-home moms choose is to become experts at penny-pinching. When a friend of Luke's, whose mother worked full time, got an ATV, Luke was jealous. "I wish I could get something like that, Mom. But I never will because you don't work outside the home." (Actually, I was working part-time during school hours, three or four days a week when he said that.) Before I could say anything, his friend replied, "I'd rather have my mom home than an ATV. I never see her." And this was from a fourteen-year-old boy.

It's hard to nurture emotional intimacy and passion in a relationship when you are constantly fighting and complaining about money. If your husband is the "spendaholic," get educated and take steps to steer things in the right direction. If you're the one living beyond your means, pray for contentment and for wisdom on why you overspend. Having lived paycheck to paycheck for most of our marriage, I know that having margin in our finances as we do now definitely puts less stress on our relationship. It allows Stu to be the generous guy he likes to be, and I don't have a meltdown over every expenditure.

In Sickness and in Health

We all know which condition—sickness or health—any of us prefer. If given the choice, would any of us ever choose sickness? Of course not. But we don't live in a perfect world, and various illnesses and health issues serve to decrease sizzle in a marriage. Tearful women have confided in me that fertility problems or miscarriages have adversely affected their passion and romance. Immature spouses leave when the going gets tough. One dear woman in a Bible study I taught was diagnosed with breast cancer. After her mastectomy, her husband said, "I didn't sign up for this" and left. I also read about a wife who took their young daughter and left her husband when he was injured and confined to a wheelchair. Physical illness is not pretty, and because it's our human nature to avoid unpleasantness, remaining true "in sickness" is included in the vows. A marriage may sizzle in health but grow even deeper and stronger in sickness.

Emotional illness can impact marriages as well. Many times over the course of a marriage, one spouse will change. It's important not to minimize the impact this can have on a relationship, especially on the spouse who hasn't changed. Even good changes can cause differences. If your spouse has been codependent, overweight, alcoholic, addicted, or abusive—and you always thought things would be great if only he quit that behavior—it can still be upsetting when roles shift and what used to work doesn't anymore. Change is hard at first, but embracing the positive strides your spouse has made will benefit you, too.

Forsaking All Others

"Forsaking all others" means giving up everyone else for the sake of your spouse. God instructs us in Genesis, "a man will leave his father and mother and be united to his wife" (2:24). This is the first step in creating marital oneness. Both a husband and wife must cut the apron strings with their parents in order to build a close, loving relationship.

When you promised your husband you would forsake all others, you also closed the door on ever entertaining the option of another love interest, whether in real life or over the Internet. I heard once that being true to the covenant of your marriage means forgoing any relationship in which you find greater emotional satisfaction or delight than in your spouse. That's a clear filter to run all our relationships through, not just those with the opposite sex.

I know how tempting it is to fill your inner and outer life with people who bring you pleasure instead of pain, especially when you are in a difficult space with your husband. If you are currently struggling, please go back to chapter 5. Reread the section on emotional attachments and pray the prayer of separation. If you're involved in an actual affair, please stop. For the sake of your marriage, your family, your relationship with the Lord, His reputation, and any ministry He would like to accomplish through you, I am pleading with you to forsake all others for your husband.

> A key to staying happily married for a lifetime is trying to do at least one thing every day to make your marriage sizzle.

With My Body, I Thee Worship

This beautiful phrase is rarely used in weddings today. Yet, more than any other promise we make, I believe it captures the depth of intimacy and oneness God intended for marriage. The act of worship, which is part of an intimate love relationship with God, is expanded to include showing adoration to our spouse through the sexual relationship.

Do you worship your husband with your body, or do you withhold? Are you giving your body freely to him without reservation? Do both of you strive to make the other feel appreciated and adored in the bedroom? "In God's design, sex and an intimate marriage can never be separated."[5] It doesn't matter what a great wife you are in every other area of your marriage—fabulous cook, fastidious housecleaner, devoted mother, financial whiz, even physically attractive. If you aren't dedicated to expressing love to your husband through your sexual relationship—worshipping him with your body—you won't experience the full range of intimacy and passion your union was designed for.

From This Day Forward

"Getting married is easy. Staying married is more difficult. Staying happily married for a lifetime would be considered among the fine arts."[6] A key to staying happily married for a lifetime is trying to do at least one thing every day to make your marriage sizzle. Now before you throw down the book and say, "That's impossible!" remember I challenged you in chapter 6 to consider making your relationship with your husband the second priority in life, right after your relationship with Jesus Christ.

Practically, though, how does a busy wife and mother do this? Again, the answer is simple but not easy. You start ordering your days with your beloved in mind. First, make sure you are spending regular time with God in His Word, prayer, and worship. Then do one thing you know would be meaningful to your husband and which would strengthen your marriage that day. How do you know what that one thing is? Ask him. Maybe he'd just like his lunch made that morning, or perhaps he wants you to reserve some energy for him that night. It could be balancing the checkbook because you're better at accounting than he is, or greeting him at the door with a big hug and kiss.

A young wife told me recently one of the tips she got out of my "Sizzle" talk is that she now makes their bed every day so the master bedroom looks beautiful and feels like a love nest for her and her husband. *Focus on the Family* magazine suggested couples should "talk together every day, pray and kiss passionately."[7] As I've said elsewhere in the

Make your relationship with your husband second only to your relationship with Jesus Christ.

book, become an expert on your man and let him know how much he means to you by making him a priority. Do at least one thing each day that shows he's important to you; don't just give him your leftovers.

"From this day forward" also means you can't rewrite the past, but you can determine in your heart and with God's help to begin each day asking God to fill you with a fresh love for your husband. Address the concerns that make your marriage unpleasant, and accept what will probably never change, as long as it's not harmful to you or your children.

We usually associate the "Serenity Prayer" with alcoholic and other recovery programs, and many of us are familiar only with the first four lines. But the other day I ran across the entire prayer in a book and was profoundly touched. No matter what our circumstances in life, each of us could benefit from living by its words.

The Serenity Prayer

God, grant me the serenity

to accept the things I cannot change,

the courage to change the things I can,

and the wisdom to know the difference.

Living one day at a time;

enjoying one moment at a time;

accepting hardship as a pathway to peace;

taking, as Jesus did,

this sinful world as it is,

not as I would have it;

trusting that you will make all things right

if I surrender to your will;

so that I may be reasonably happy in this life

and supremely happy with you forever in the next.

Reinhold Niebuhr

What God Has Joined Together

In Ecclesiastes we read, "A cord of three strands is not quickly broken" (4:12). Many Christian couples use this verse in their wedding ceremony because the accepted interpretation implies the three strands are you, your husband, and God. A union with God at the center should improve our character so that "a man and a woman become more richly themselves together than the chances are either of them could ever have managed to become alone."[8]

But what if you or your spouse aren't connected to the

wonderful, powerful God of the universe and are trying to make your marriage work without Him? Some couples appear to keep their relationship together and stable without depending on the Lord. To these capable individuals I would say, given the strength of your relationship, can you imagine how much deeper it could be and what a blessing you would be to others if you invited God into your marriage? Then there are the rest of us who doubt we'd still be married if God wasn't at the center of our lives every single day.

One of the most touching moments I ever experienced in the years of sharing my "Sizzle" talk happened last May. I was speaking in Denver, and everything was going wrong. It was one of those mornings when I couldn't get through my talk fast enough so I could console myself over lunch with a friend. As I sat at the book-signing table, a young woman approached me with tears in her eyes and asked if we could talk privately.

As soon as we sat down, Kara said, "Denise, I don't think I'm a Christian like you talk about being a Christian." She then poured her heart out for the next half hour about her marriage woes, which were significant. When she was done, I took her hand and said, "First, let's talk about your comment that you don't think you're a Christian." I explained that a Christian is someone who realizes she needs the forgiveness of Jesus Christ in her life, and that only through Him can she have a relationship with God. I finished by asking, "Do you understand?" She looked at me, shook her head, and honestly replied, "Not really."

God's direct intervention clearly guided the next part of our conversation. I knew Kara had a two-year-old boy, Taylor, who was everything to her. So I began again.

"Kara, Taylor means the world to you, doesn't he?"

"Yes," she quietly said and nodded.

"Would you do as much for your neighbor's children as you do for Taylor?"

She replied, "No. They aren't my flesh and blood."

I nodded in agreement and went on to say, "Kara, when we are not connected to God through faith in His Son, Jesus Christ, we are like that neighbor's children in His eyes. We aren't family. Kara, I want God to be able to do everything He desires for you and your husband, but until you know Him through His Son, you aren't 'family' to Him, and He can't do as much for you as He would like."

There's a measure of comfort to be found in knowing God handpicks your specific trials and pleasures in order for you to grow into the mature, beautiful woman He longs for you to be.

At this point I asked her once again if she understood what it meant to be a Christian, and she said, "Yes, I do." I then had the privilege of asking her if she would like to pray and ask Jesus Christ to be her Lord and Savior so she could be connected to God and part of His family forever. We bowed our heads and prayed for her sins to be forgiven. Then we asked Christ to come into her heart to be her Lord and Savior.

Kara's soul was saved that day for all eternity, and I hope her marriage was too.

God had an appointment that day with Kara so she could become one of His children, and she didn't even know it. Perhaps today He's waiting to keep a similar appointment with you.

Till Death Us Do Part

Well, we've reached the end of our book as well as the last portion of our vows. When you stood as a starry-eyed bride at the altar with your handsome groom, you probably couldn't have imagined all your life together would hold in the years ahead— joyful, ecstatic times, as well as hard ones. There's a measure of comfort to be found in knowing God handpicks your specific trials and pleasures in order for you to grow into the mature, beautiful woman He longs for you to be.

When we marry, none of us knows for sure how long our union will last. We hope we'll spend the sunset of our lives growing old with our beloved. And many of us will be blessed with exactly that. But the truth is, death may interrupt at any time. Sometimes with warning, as in the case of terminal illness, other times without any preparation at all. When it does come, as it will to all of us, wouldn't you like to know deep in your heart that you had no regrets where your relationship with your husband was concerned? Let me close with the true story of a young wife whose marriage ended too quickly, but without regrets.

A Marriage with No Regrets

Our three gorgeous nieces live in Oklahoma. They are not only physically beautiful but spiritually lovely as well. Talented (they all sing like angels), athletic (they all play basketball), and hard working, these young women are delightful in every way.

When she was nineteen, Stephanie, the middle sister, surprised everyone when she became engaged to a wonderful man six years her senior, Tekon McCune. Tekon already owned his own contracting business, had built the three-bedroom house he lived in right out of high school, and was a popular leader among the youth at church. Furthermore, this godly man had never had a girlfriend or even kissed a girl until he met Stephanie. Tekon and Stephanie had eyes only for each other, and their springtime ceremony was everything a wedding should be. They happily began married life with few of the adjustments common to many newlyweds.

Fast forward to June 2004. Tekon, Stephanie, and her sisters joined our family at our favorite vacation spot in Missouri: Tablerock Lake. Stephanie was seven months pregnant and glowing. Tekon was as solicitous as ever toward his young wife, helping her in and out of the boat, always making sure she was comfortable, tenderly acting the way every woman dreams her husband will, especially when she is pregnant.

After four days of waterskiing, shopping for the baby, playing games, and eating barbecue together, we all met on their last day at a site on the lake known for its spectacular cliff jumps. More than twenty boats sat anchored in the cove as families swam near the cliffs and picnicked on their boats. The sun shone brightly, and we could hear shouts of laughter and applause every time someone successfully landed a jump in the dark blue water.

When a few brave souls from our group announced they were going to jump from the cliffs, Tekon joined them. Stephanie confided he always was a bit of a daredevil—and had ended up in the hospital several times with concussions due to his antics. We assured her nothing like that would happen. People jumped from the cliffs every day, and we had never heard of anyone getting hurt.

Stephanie sat, camcorder in hand, on the bow of their boat. She didn't want to miss recording one second of Tekon's jump. Right before he jumped, she looked at me and said, "Aunt Denise, the camcorder won't work and I don't know why. I made sure the battery was charged. Oh well, I guess I'll have to settle for taking a picture with the still camera instead."

At that moment, we heard Tekon call out, "Are you ready, Steph?"

"I'm ready, baby," she shouted back.

As Tekon sailed through the air, I noticed he was bent at a forty-five-degree angle and wondered why, since you want to enter the water as upright as possible. I was a little concerned, but an out-of-shape, middle-aged man had landed in a funny position a few jumps earlier and was perfectly fine, so I wasn't too worried.

When Tekon hit the water, you could hear the collective "Ow-w-w," the sound everyone made if a landing looked bad. Because he had a life jacket on, he popped out of the water for a moment. Then he fell forward, facedown in the lake, and lay there unmoving. In an instant, the entire cove went completely silent. The seconds ticked by as Tekon remained facedown in the water until Stephanie began screaming, "Someone help him! Someone help him!" She scrambled out of the boat, over the foot of the cliffs, jumped into the lake and began swimming toward him.

Two doctors and a registered nurse were on other boats in the cove that day. They immediately made their way to the boat Tekon was taken to and began CPR. Paramedics met us on shore and continued to try to revive him, but to no avail. Tekon had died instantly, and a sweet, God-honoring marriage that should have lasted a lifetime and was such a blessing to so many, came to an abrupt end.

Several days later, as I held Stephanie in my arms and let her cry, she looked at me and said, "Aunt Denise, the night before we left on vacation, did you know Tekon and I spent more than five hours going through a book Rachel [her sister] had given us called *Just the Two of Us*? We told each other everything two people in love would want to. In the two weeks before he died, several things happened like that. In fact, Tekon lived every day with me that way. Every night, before we went to sleep, he took me in his arms and said, 'Thank you for marrying me.'

"If anyone else I cared about had died, I would have had regrets about not saying or doing everything I had wanted to for them before they died. I'm so grateful I don't have any regrets with Tekon."

After reading Stephanie's story, I pray you are willing to do all in your power to live out a marriage with no regrets. Not a perfect marriage but a relationship where emotional intimacy and passion are nurtured and grow because you've given your all to love, honor, and cherish the man God has given you.

God bless you as you live out these secrets to make your marriage sizzle.

Afterword

This is a personal note to the woman who has read this book, tried with all her heart to implement the seven secrets, and yet has met with defeat or a lukewarm response at best from her husband. Please understand that the tips and teachings I've written about work best for wives in committed, stable marriages. One of my greatest concerns is that a reader will feel like a failure as a wife because the ideas presented here haven't improved her marriage.

If your husband is enmeshed in or controlled by addiction, abuse, or an adulterous relationship, the "secrets" I've shared simply won't apply. These encouragements and helps are for the average marriage that may have slipped a little (or a lot) due to neglect, difficult seasons in life, boredom, or stagnation and just needs some guidance and motivation to get it going in the right direction.

This said, it is doubtful my book will be of much help to a deeply distressed marriage. Prayer, godly counsel, educating yourself on the source of the problem or problems, deciding on a plan of action, and the loving support of mature Christians are all essential to dealing with a dysfunctional marriage. Our wonderful God is more than faithful. He hears every cry of our heart and answers us as we seek to know and fulfill His highest will for our lives. If you are in a painful marriage, may the Lord bless and keep you as you find the strength to initiate change and move toward healing in your relationship.

In Christ's love,
Denise Vezey

QUESTIONS FOR COUPLES

1. If you received $5,000 as a gift, how would you spend it?
2. If you could live any place in the world, where would it be?
3. Of all the material possessions you have, which one gives you the most pleasure?
4. What TV show would you like to star in?
5. What do you think about when you can't fall asleep?
6. What would you like to invent to make life better?
7. If you wrote a book, what would the title be?
8. If you could have been someone famous in history, who would it have been?
9. If you were lost in the woods at night, what would you do?
10. What do you like to do in your spare time?
11. What is something you do well?
12. Share one of the happiest days of your life.
13. What do you like most about yourself?
14. What do you like least?
15. What would you like to be remembered for after you die?
16. In one sentence, how would you describe what life is all about?
17. How would you define peace?
18. What makes you feel sad?

19. When were you most embarrassed and why?
20. What is something that really bugs you?
21. When you are alone and no one can see or hear you, what do you like to do?
22. What do you think makes a happy marriage?
23. What four things are most important in your life?
24. How would you describe heaven?
25. What was a big disappointment in your life?
26. If you could change your age, what age would you like to be?
27. How would you describe the best teacher you've ever had?
28. What was a turning point in your life?
29. What makes a house a home?
30. What advice would you give a young man or woman about to be married?
31. How would you complete the statement "Words can't describe how I felt when ..."?
32. What is your ideal life?
33. What things make your life complicated?
34. What are three things you're thankful for?
35. What feelings do you have the most trouble expressing?
36. What is your favorite name for God?
37. What activity do you engage in that involves your heart, mind, and soul?
38. What spiritual goal are you reaching for?
39. How do you experience God's presence?
40. What is your favorite hymn or worship song?
41. When did you last feel God led you?
42. Can you tell me about a time when your feelings were hurt?
43. What do you fear the most?
44. What is one of your favorite memories?
45. How would you describe your life right now?

46. What lifetime dream would you like to see come true?
47. If you had to move and could only take three things with you, what would they be?
48. What is your favorite room in your house and why?
49. What talent do you wish you had?
50. How do you define courage?
51. Who is someone you consider courageous?
52. If you could travel anywhere in the world, where would you go?
53. What do you like to daydream about?
54. If someone wrote a book about you, what would it be titled?
55. What accomplishment are you most proud of in life?
56. Can you share one thing in which you feel like a failure?
57. If you could go back in time and change one aspect of your life, what would it be?
58. What makes you happy?
59. How would you spend the perfect day?
60. What is the first question you want to ask God when you get to heaven?
61. What character in the Bible do you relate to?
62. When did you last feel particularly close to God?
63. How has God answered your prayers recently?
64. When did you really help somebody?
65. What is your favorite game?
66. What is your favorite pastime?
67. What is your favorite quote or Bible verse?
68. What color do you think of when you think of love?
69. What part of the Bible is difficult for you to understand?
70. What do you think your friends say about you when you're not around?
71. If you could change one thing about yourself, what would it be, and why?

72. Have you ever felt disappointed with God?
73. What is one of your favorite memories about our marriage?
74. How would you complete the statement "I feel loved when ...."?
75. What are your hopes and dreams for our relationship?
76. Has there been a time when I've let you down?
77. When do you feel most vulnerable?
78. What is the hardest thing you've ever done?
79. What epitaph do you want on your gravestone?
80. If you had only one week to live, how would you spend it?
81. If you could have a better relationship with one person, who would that be?
82. What phrase or saying really encourages you?
83. Who has had a positive influence on your life? Why?
84. What recent accomplishment is important to you?
85. Can you share a time you had victory over sin?
86. Who are six people you love to be with and why?
87. What is the title of your favorite book?
88. How can I be more of a blessing in your life?
89. How can I be a better wife/husband to you?
90. How can I be a better lover to you?

Resources

Abortion

Organizations
Care Net, 109 Carpenter Dr., Ste. 100, Sterling, VA 20164, (703) 478-5661, E-mail: Carenet@erols.com

Women Exploited by Abortion (WEBA), PO Box 278, Dawson, TX 76639

Video
After the Choice, Concerned Women for America, 800-527-9600

Adultery

Books
Boundaries in Marriage, Henry Cloud and John Townsend (Grand Rapids, MI: Zondervan, 1999)

Love Must Be Tough, James Dobson (Nashville: Word, 1983)

Unfaithful, Gary and Mona Shriver (Colorado Springs: Cook, 2005)

Counseling
Focus on the Family Counseling Department, 1-800-A-FAMILY

Pornography

Organizations
National Coalition Against Pornography, 800 Compton Rd., Ste. 9224, Cincinnati, OH 45231, (513) 521-6227

Pure Life Ministries, PO Box 410, Dry Ridge, KY 41035, (606) 824-4444

Books
> *An Affair of the Mind,* Laurie Hall (Colorado Springs: Focus
> on the Family Publishing, 1996)
> *False Intimacy: Understanding the Struggle of Sexual
> Addictions,* Harry Schaumburg (Colorado Springs:
> NavPress, 1992)
> *Pornography: A Human Tragedy,* Tom Minnery (Wheaton,
> IL: Tyndale House, 1987)

Sexual Abuse

Organizations
> Freedom in Christ Ministries, Dr. Neil Anderson, 10 West
> Dry Creek Cir., Littleton, CO 80120, (303) 730-4211
> Wounded Heart Ministries, Dr. Dan Allender, (888) 977-
> 2002

Books
> *The Wounded Heart,* Dr. Dan Allender (Colorado Springs:
> NavPress, 1990)

Counseling
> Focus on the Family, (800) A-FAMILY
> New Life Clinics (800) NEW-LIFE
> The Rape Abuse Incest National Network Hotline, 1-800-
> 656-HOPE

Tapes
> *Healing Childhood Traumas,* the story of Stephanie Fast,
> Focus on the Family, (800) A-FAMILY, tapes CS298

I also recommend contacting your church or pastor to ask
about local therapists trained in biblical counseling with expertise in particular issues.

Readers' Guide

for Personal Reflection or
Group Discussion

Readers' Guide

These days we can't help raising an eyebrow when we hear a couple has been married for twenty-five years. We see relationships crumble around us all the time—marriages between people full of bitterness and marriages between people who are good and pleasant, marriages that should still be in the honeymoon phase and marriages that seemed to have existed before time.

In the midst of this, it is sometimes difficult to remain optimistic about your own marriage. You are all too aware of the differences between you and your husband and find it difficult to remember what originally attracted you. You may even wonder if it is worth the effort to try to make it work.

I want to assure you that it is—not only to avoid the pain of divorce or to develop your character through selfless perseverance, not only to bless those around you by giving them a model of integrity—but also that you may experience the fullness of what God intends for your marriage.

Mustering up hope during times of despair is nearly impossible to do alone. Surround yourself with Christian women who will walk with you and you with them, so that you may encourage each other to continue to hope.

"May the God of hope fill you with all joy and peace as you trust in him, so that you may overflow with hope by the power of the Holy Spirit" (Rom. 15:13).

The guide that follows offers several options for study. If your husband is interested in what you've been reading, you can direct him to the "For Husbands Only" sections. For times of personal study, work through the "For Your Eyes Only" sections.

If the two of you want to work together on issues facing your marriage, do the activities in the "For Lovers Only" sections. Of course, you can also reflect on the "For Your Group" questions on your own, as a couple, or in a small-group setting. May God enrich your lives as you seek His best for your marriage.

Secret 1: Let Go of Perfection

For Husbands Only

If your wife gets a little cranky and doesn't act perfectly romantic before you make love, don't take it personally. She may be letting off steam, like a teakettle, so she doesn't explode. Enjoy the gift of herself that she's offering, and, if you really want to score points, ask her afterward if she wants to talk about anything.

For Your Eyes Only

If you could change one thing about your husband, what would it be? Write your answer down on a separate piece of paper.

Offer your desire up to the Lord, asking Him to change either your husband in this area or to change your heart, whichever would please God most. Think of one word that will trigger you to be faithful to continue praying until you sense God has answered. Finally, throw away or burn your secret request.

For Lovers Only

The next time you and your husband have an unresolved issue, ask the Lord to help you put aside the matter and be a warm and available sexual partner for your husband. You may even want to initiate lovemaking, which will probably really surprise him!

Afterward, if it seems appropriate, either gently bring up the issue that's been bothering you (if it still exists), or ask your husband to share an area in which he feels you expect too much from him. Tell him about an area you think he expects perfection from you. End by reassuring him you don't want unrealistic expectations to be an issue between you.

For You and Your Group

1. Share one character strength of your husband that has greatly enhanced your marriage.

2. Which of the four areas mentioned in chapter 1 are most difficult for you as a wife: letting go of expectations, agreeably adapting, forgiving your husband, or praising God for your husband and your marriage?

3. Decide on one step you will take this week to improve your marriage, and then tell the group about your decision. For example, if managing expectations is difficult for you, you could begin with Stormie Omartian's prayer, quoted in chapter 1, in which you release your husband from your expectations and lay them at the cross of Christ. If it is adapting, you might ask the Lord to show you one area in which you will actively try to be more agreeable. If it is forgiveness, ask the Lord to help you pray to forgive your husband if he has been hurtful in your marriage or family. If you need to praise God for your husband and your marriage, commit to spending at least five minutes every day doing just that.

4. Read Colossians 3:12–15 several times this week and answer the following questions:

    a. How do the qualities listed here coincide with the four areas mentioned in question two?

    b. Describe a time in your life that holds particular meaning for you, when God displayed one or more of these attributes toward you. God, through the Holy Spirit, is more than willing to help you display these attributes toward your husband, as you ask Him.

5. Close by spending time praising God for every husband

and marriage represented there. Have each woman thank God out loud for her husband's strengths and admirable character qualities, as well as the gift of being married.

Secret 2: Language of Lovers

For Husbands Only

If you don't know your wife's primary and secondary love languages, make a point to find out. Speak her language at least once a week for one month and watch your love life heat up!

For Your Eyes Only

Make a list of all the times your husband has been a romantic disappointment to you. Perhaps he never brings you flowers or forgot your anniversary. Write down whatever has caused you hurt or heartache. Next, go before the Lord and pray to forgive your husband for every offense. Whether he hurt you out of ignorance or indifference, let go of your man's romantic failings and start fresh. Repeat this exercise at least once a month for the rest of your lives together.

For Lovers Only

If you and your husband have never discussed the five love languages, carve out some time to help him see how understanding and speaking one another's love language can keep the intimacy and passion in your marriage going strong. If you already know one another's language, make this a lighthearted "reminder" meeting.

Each of you should write down all five languages and then rank them in order of importance to you. Do this even if you think you already know one another's love languages because priorities may have changed. Then trade lists and talk about how each of you would like your love language expressed. For example, if your husband's primary love language is meaningful time, ask him to describe in detail how that would look to him.

Would it be talking every night for twenty minutes after dinner? A date night for just the two of you—no kids or other couples allowed—every Friday night so he can count on having time alone with you? Let your mate, not you, define what feels like love.

Make an effort to speak each other's primary love language at least once a week.

For You and Your Group

1. Share with your group your top two love languages. Remember, love languages are for friends and other family members as well, so you may want to take notes!

2. By a show of hands, find out how many women share the same primary love language as their husbands.

3. Brainstorm with your group several different ways each love language can be expressed. Write down ideas so you can refer to them later.

4. Read Philippians 2:1–11 throughout the week and answer the following questions:

   a. How is selfishness detrimental to emotional intimacy and passion in a marriage?

   b. How has Christ been unselfish toward us? With Christ as our example, He can show us how to be unselfish and look out for our husband's interests, not just our own.

5. Pray that the Lord would help you speak your husband's love language on a consistent basis and that your husband would have a heart willing to show love in ways that are meaningful to you.

Secret 3: Laugh and Play

For Husbands Only

Ask your wife to name the three favorite activities she enjoys with you. Find time in your schedule to do at least one a month. If you really want to make your marriage sizzle, surprise her by doing all the planning: buy tickets, arrange for a sitter, check her calendar. Do whatever it takes to show her you're looking forward to your time with her.

For Your Eyes Only

Are there any recreational activities your husband likes to do that you don't enjoy? If so, make a list and note why each is unpleasant to you. Does it take too much time away from you or the children? Is it expensive? Is it boring?

For Lovers Only

Ask your husband which activity he would most like you to participate in and how often he wants you with him. If he wants you to take part in a sport you are unfamiliar with, discuss the possibility of taking lessons, what kind of equipment you'd need, and so forth. Show enthusiasm for his choice, and commit to taking part!

For You and Your Group

1. Share with the group what season of marriage you and your husband find yourselves in—spring, summer, autumn, or winter—and why you are there. Discuss whether it's easy or difficult for you to be your husband's recreational companion during this time and what factors in your life make it this way.

2. Take turns telling the group about your favorite memory of a time you and your husband spent laughing and playing together. Talk about what recreational activity you now enjoy most with him and which you enjoy least or don't participate in.

3. Read Ecclesiastes 3:1–11 several times during the week and answer the following questions:

    a. What do these verses say about recognizing the need for balance in our lives?

b. Does God have an appropriate time for all that takes place in our lives?

c. How do balance and time issues impact your marriage? If we truly seek God's will for our lives with an obedient heart, He will help us order our days and take care of all we are responsible for no matter what season of marriage we are in.

4. Pray for women struggling with obstacles that stop them from becoming their husband's recreational companion. Pray that each woman in your group would rediscover the joy and laughter, emotional closeness and bonding that come from making time for fun in her marriage.

Secret 4: Life's Little Luxuries

For Husbands Only

Be a sweetie and make your wife's "dream date" come true this month. Plan the entire day, evening, or weekend—including childcare—and watch your wife come alive in response to the warmth of your love and care for her.

For Your Eyes Only

Ask the Lord to show you which luxury would benefit your marriage most at this time: emotional privacy, physical privacy, dating, or a weekend away. Next, if you know you haven't put much effort into a certain area, ask God to forgive you and to help you grow.

If you've neglected to provide emotional privacy for your husband, you may need to become more trustworthy or more transparent. If you're lacking physical privacy, you may need to make practical changes around your home or strive to be more spontaneous.

If you're not dating your husband, make the first move to reestablish time together and be creative. If you've resisted going away, put your worries and fears aside and say yes.

On a favorite piece of stationery, take a few moments to write out a statement to God and your husband describing your renewed commitment to emotional intimacy and passion in your marriage. It might look like this:

> Dear Lord,
>
> Thank You for giving my husband, _____, to me. Too often our relationship is a gift we both take for granted. Please help us to grow more loving toward one another, so we can experience the emotional intimacy and passion You designed us for. In particular, I want to commit to being a wife who is pleasing to You—emotionally, physically, spiritually, and mentally—and especially one who brings pleasure to my husband through the everyday luxuries You've provided. Open my eyes to all You've given us and my heart toward all You want me to be.
>
> Signed,
>
> (Your Name)
>
> (and Date)

Finally, a few days before you do the For Lovers Only assignment, ask the Lord to prepare both your hearts for your meeting and for gentle and receptive spirits. (Life tip: Everything goes better with prayer!)

For Lovers Only

Set aside at least one hour to discuss the four luxuries: emotional privacy, physical privacy, dates, and weekends away. Ask your husband which luxury he would like to see more of in your marriage. If he seems less than enthusiastic about a particular luxury, ask if he's been hurt by you in this area. Ask his forgiveness and assure him you are trying to make a fresh commitment to intimacy and passion in your relationship.

If you are the one who has been hurt, gently bring up why you've been reluctant to make privacy, dating, or time alone away a priority. It may also help if you tell him what he could do to inspire you to be a more willing participant in the little luxuries of marriage.

Finally, if you haven't talked about your three favorite dates for the next three months, now's the time to do it—and close your meeting on a positive note.

For You and Your Group

1. Tell the group which luxury is needed most in your marriage at this time: emotional privacy, physical privacy, dates, or a weekend away. What makes it difficult for you and your husband to take advantage of this built-in luxury? A lack of money? Time? The phase of life you're in? Do you think these obstacles are temporary or permanent?

2. Share an experience from one of the four categories mentioned above that has worked well for you. Write these ideas down as future possibilities for you and your husband.

3. Read Philippians 4:4–9, 19 several times this week.

　　a. What does God promise in verse 19? Discuss in your group the different needs many of you are facing.

　　b. Can anyone share a time when God fulfilled His promise of supplying all your needs? Do you think God is talking about just the necessities of life here? Why or why not?

4. The same God who brought you and your husband together cares deeply that your relationship remains loving and strong. As you seek Him and make a fresh commitment in your heart to your husband, you can trust that He will "liberally supply" everything you need, whether it be finances, baby-sitters, or unscheduled time, so your marriage can succeed.

Pray for any needs, spoken or unspoken, you would like to

see God supply. Thank Him for promising to take care of us in the future and for the times He already has.

Secret 5: Liberated for Love

For Husbands Only

Allow your wife to explain the concepts presented in this chapter. Then, if necessary, pray whichever prayers apply to you, either alone or with your wife. Afterward, invite your wife to celebrate your newfound freedom with a special night of special intimacy.

For Your Eyes Only

If you haven't done so already, pray the prayers that relate to you. If you did but haven't felt the release and sense of freedom you expected, get together with a female friend or mentor and ask her if she would pray these prayers with you, agreeing in the Spirit that what God promises, He will do.

For Lovers Only

Sit across from one another on your bed. Hold hands and look into each other's eyes. One at a time, ask each other's forgiveness for every area of sexual sin that has hindered your physical, emotional, and spiritual intimacy.

For each offense you or your spouse asks forgiveness for, say out loud, "I forgive you." Take as much time as you need to adequately forgive, and discuss any issue that needs further attention. Again, you may want to celebrate your newfound closeness with a night of special intimacy.

This exercise may feel awkard for both of you, but it can be a sweet and healing time of closure.

For You and Your Group

1. Because of the nature of this chapter, it may not be comfortable or appropriate to share in your group specifically how the material presented helped you. Instead, take some time to

anonymously write down which prayers or chapter sections applied to you. Was it sexual contact outside of marriage? An inappropriate emotional attachment? Divorce or sexual abuse, including rape? Forgiveness, counseling, or addressing physical problems?

Sit in a circle and put all the pieces of paper in the center. Have your group leader read them out loud. Many times we feel we're the only ones hiding an awful secret of our sexual past or present. A measure of comfort can be found in knowing God forgives, works, and heals in all of our lives, and we are not alone as we struggle.

2. Ask for feedback on what the group thought of the ideas presented in this chapter. Did they make sense? Did they seem far-fetched? It's healthy to dialogue about concepts that aren't familiar to us. Try to keep in mind the old Protestant saying during the discussion: "In essentials, unity. In nonessentials, liberty. In all things charity." Avoid a contentious or argumentative atmosphere.

This chapter has the potential to be emotionally difficult for many readers. Be especially sensitive to anyone who may be troubled or hurting. Let the group minister to one another from the insights God has shown them and any stories of healing they would be willing to share. Allow for an extended time of prayer and support instead of a more structured discussion.

3. Read Isaiah 61:1–3 several times during the week in different translations if possible. Then answer the following questions:

    a. Who is "me" in verse one? (If you are unsure, look up Luke 4:14–20.)

    b. Are you glad there will be a "day of vengeance of our God"? Why or why not?

    c. How would you describe "oaks of righteousness"?

d. Which promises from these verses are meaningful to
   you?

4. Praise God verse by verse through Isaiah 61:1–3 for who
He promises to be in our lives. For example, "Lord Jesus, I praise
You that You were sent to care for and bind up all who are brokenhearted. We pray for any women in our group today, and
others we know, who are hurting from a heart that's been broken. May they truly know You as the one who heals." Then
praise Him for announcing liberty for the captives, and so forth
until every verse that contains a promise is covered.

Secret 6: Lighten Up!

For Husbands Only

Women are responders. Believe it or not, you hold the power
to make your wife want to be with you more on every level, in
every way. If she is shy in the bedroom, pour on the compliments. Tell her how much you love her body and how happy
she makes you. Regular doses of admiration should help even
the most inhibited wife unless deeper issues or problems need to
be addressed.

For Your Eyes Only

On two separate pieces of paper, write down everything you
like or dislike about your sexual relationship with your husband,
using one sheet for each. When you are done, put the positive
paper aside. Take the paper filled with negatives and review each
one before the Lord. Ask Him to show you which attitudes are
legitimate and which ones need work. Also, decide which dis-
likes are your responsibility and which ones are your husband's.
Could you lovingly speak to him about any of them?

For instance, if you don't like making love because you're
always tired, try taking a nap in the afternoon or paying attention to your body's cycles. Then make the most of those times

when you do have energy. Or, if you dislike a certain way your husband touches you during lovemaking, instead of silently seething, you could gently suggest he try something different.

For Lovers Only

Prayerfully pick one concept from this chapter that you think would help your sexual relationship the most. Ask your husband to set aside a few moments for an uninterrupted conversation with you. Positive list in hand, begin your time together by telling him all the things you enjoy or appreciate about your physical relationship. It's also nice to ask him what he likes best about you in that area. Next, share with him the tip you feel would increase your desire for one another. Does he agree? Is he willing to give it a try?

If growing in your sexual relationship involves a more serious issue, decide beforehand what boundaries need to be set if there is an unwillingness to stop an offending behavior. Speaking the truth in love without attacking can be effective, especially when coupled with firm lines of respect and prayer.

For You and Your Group

1. Ask the group to say on a scale of one to ten—with one being scared silly and ten being wild and crazy—how adventurous are you in your physical relationship with your husband? Where do you want to be? Then discuss how the special husband assignment in the section, "Take a Deep Breath," went. If you opted not to do it, explain why.

2. Discuss which concept in this chapter would help you personally "lighten up" the most. Relationship meetings? Responding to your husband's lead? Acting on his request for fun? Making a "creative memory"? Losing weight or getting in shape? Share as briefly or as in-depth as you would like.

3. Read Genesis 2:18–25 several times this week in different translations, then out loud in your group when you meet

together. As you read these verses, ask yourself the following questions:

    a. What does it mean to be a "suitable helper"?

    b. Are you more of a helpmate or a hindrance to your husband? What would he say if you asked him the question?

    c. Why do you think physical intimacy, not just emotional intimacy, between a husband and wife is important to God (v. 24)?

    d. God's intention for all married couples is clear in verse 25: "The man and his wife were both naked, and they felt no shame." What would it take for this original ideal to be recaptured in your marriage?

4. Nothing is too private for you to share with the Lord. He made you and your husband, and He created the institution of marriage as a safeguard for all His children. Ask Him specifically for whatever it is you need in your relationship with your husband and trust that He hears you and that He is able to do "immeasurably more than all we ask or imagine, according to his power that is at work within us" (Eph. 3:20).

Pray that every wife in your group would be motivated to reenergize the sexual relationship with her husband and to give her marriage top priority, right after her commitment to Jesus Christ. If deep-seated problems are blocking the way, ask God to move in a powerful way so the marriages in your group can be healed and saved.

Secret 7: Loyalty for a Lifetime

For Husbands Only

On one of your milestone anniversaries, or if you've just come through a particularly rough year, surprise your wife with a private ceremony to renew your wedding vows and present her with an anniversary ring or a second honeymoon. Tell her, if given the choice, you'd marry her all over again. It will mean the world to her!

For Your Eyes Only

Think back to your wedding day. Has your marriage exceeded your expectations, met your ideals, or fallen short? This is between you and God only.

If your relationship has been better than you imagined it would be, spend time thanking and praising Him for the incredible blessing of a strong, loving union.

If it has been exactly what you thought it would be, thank the Lord for no major difficulties and ask Him what you can do, perhaps from this book, to take your relationship to the next level.

If your marriage has been a huge disappointment, thank God for everything you can think of that is good about your husband and your relationship, and praise Him for how you've grown through the trials. Confess any sinfulness on your part that has contributed to the problems in your marriage; then ask the Lord to give you the wisdom and strength you need to initiate positive change in your marriage.

For Lovers Only

Tell your husband you are planning a special night for the two of you to celebrate your marriage. When the special night arrives, wear something that makes you feel beautiful. If you go out, choose a restaurant that is nostalgic for the two of you or a particularly romantic setting. If you stay home (no kids allowed!), use linen tablecloths, china, and candlelight. Play love songs that bring back sweet memories for the two of you.

Get out your wedding album and go over the pictures together. Talk about your wedding day, the honeymoon, your hopes and dreams as newlyweds, the first place you lived—anything that rekindles the fire of your love for one another.

Next, take turns sharing all the things you appreciate about the other person and how much your spouse means to you. Try not to leave anything unsaid. Wrap up the evening with a time of sexual pleasure. Enjoy!

For You and Your Group

1. Ask the women in your group to share which wedding vow was the easiest to fulfill. Which have been the most difficult? Why?

2. Discuss which secret—letting go of perfection, speaking his love language, laughing and playing with your husband, taking advantage of life's little luxuries, being liberated to love, lightening up emotionally and sexually, or loyalty for a lifetime—was already part of your marriage. On the other hand, which secret was the most helpful to you? How do you plan to keep motivated to make your marriage sizzle once you finish the book or your study is over?

3. Read Song of Songs 4:9–10 in as many translations as possible during the week. Write down your favorite, and then answer the following questions:

    a. What are some qualities of a sister? What are some qualities of a bride? Are you a better sister or bride?

    b. Would your husband say you've stolen his heart? Why or why not?

Praise God for what He has accomplished in your marriage through this book. Ask Him to continue working in a specific area that still concerns you. Close by praying this verse out loud: "Now to him who is able to do immeasurably more than all we ask or imagine, according to his power that is at work within us, to him be glory in the church and in Christ Jesus throughout all generations, for ever and ever! Amen" (Eph. 3:20–21).

Notes

Secret 1

1. *Merriam Webster's Collegiate Dictionary*, 10th ed. (Merriam-Webster, 1996), s.v. "perfection."
2. Edith Schaeffer, *Celebration of Marriage* (Grand Rapids, MI: Baker, 1994).
3. *Women's Day*, "Women That Men Love" (New York, 2001).
4. For more on temperaments and the impact they have on your marriage, I highly recommend reading *The Spirit Controlled Temperament* by Tim LaHaye (Wheaton, IL: Tyndale House, 1993).
5. Stormie Omartian, *The Power of a Praying Wife* (Eugene, OR: Harvest House, 1997), 45.
6. *Webster's New World Dictionary*, 3rd College Edition (Simon & Schuster, 1991), s.v. "adapt."
7. James Dobson quoted in Linda Dillow, *How to Really Love Your Man* (Nashville: Nelson, 1993), 29–30.

Secret 2

1. Gary Chapman, *The Five Love Languages* (Chicago: Moody Press, 1992).
2. Laura Schlessinger, *The Proper Care and Feeding of Husbands* (New York: HarperCollins, 2004), 43.
3. Jan Karon, *A Common Life: The Wedding Story* (New York: Viking Books, 2001).

4. Amy Dacyczyn, *The Tightwad Gazette* (New York: Villard Books, 1992).
5. Dr. John Gray, *Mars and Venus in the Bedroom* (New York: HarperCollins, 1995), 77.
6. Dr. Janet Wolfe, *What To Do When He Has a Headache* (New York: Hyperion, 1992).
7. Shannon Etheridge, *Every Woman's Battle* (Colorado Springs: WaterBrook Press, 2003), 144–145.
8. *Webster's New World Dictionary*, 3rd College Edition (Simon & Schuster Inc., 1989), s.v. "leech."

Secret 3

1. Willard F. Harley Jr., *His Needs, Her Needs* (Grand Rapids, MI: Fleming H. Revell, 1994), 77.
2. Gerard Manley Hopkins, *The One Year Book of Poetry* (Wheaton, IL: Tyndale House, 1999), April 29.
3. *Webster's New World Dictionary*, 3rd College Edition (Simon & Schuster Inc., 1989), s.v. "recreation."
4. Willard F. Harley Jr., *His Needs, Her Needs*, 83.

Secret 4

1. *Webster's New World Dictionary*, 3rd College Edition (Simon & Schuster, 1991), s.v. "luxury."
2. Herbert Stein, "Why a Man Needs a Woman," *Slate*, June 1997, Reprinted in *Reader's Digest*, May 2004, 150.
3. *Webster's New World Dictionary*, s.v. "Discreet."
4. Alexandra Stoddard, *Living a Beautiful Life* (New York: Avon Books, 1988).
5. Linda Dillow, *How to Really Love Your Man* (Nashville: Nelson, 1993).
6. Dave and Claudia Arp, *52 Dates for You and Your Mate* (Nashville: Nelson, 1993), 107.

Secret 5

1. U.S. Census Bureau, "Unmarried couples," www.census.gov/PressRelease/www/releases/archives. (Accessed 6/16/2005).
2. Ibid.
3. Matthew 6:14–15.
4. John and Paula Sanford, *Transformation of the Inner Man* (Tulsa: Victory House, 1982).
5. This prayer is adapted from material written by John and Paula Sanford, *The Transformation of the Inner Man*, 269–94.
6. This prayer is the author's adaptation of the previous prayer. There is no prayer for emotional attachment in the Sanfords' book.
7. Ephesians 5:25–32.
8. The adaptation of this prayer is based on the materials of Judy Myers, San José, Calif.
9. John and Paula Sanford, *Transformation of the Inner Man*, 277–311.
10. Revelation 22:12.
11. The adaptation of this prayer is based on the materials of Judy Myers, San Jose, Calif.

Secret 6

1. Linda Dillow and Lorraine Pintus, *Intimate Issues*, (Colorado Springs: WaterBrook Press, 1999), 199–210.
2. Ibid., 152.
3. Ibid., 155.
4. Ibid., 202.
5. Ibid., 202.
6. Ibid., 202.
7. Clifford and Joyce Penner, "Intimate Service," *Focus on the Family Magazine* (Colorado Springs, April 2004), 15.

8. *Reader's Digest*, "Make Love, Not Wrinkles": RD Relationships, 188.
9. *People Magazine*, "Sexiest Doctor—Mehmet Oz," (New York, Time Inc., December 2, 2002), 97.

Secret 7

1. Elisabeth Elliot, *Let Me Be a Woman* (Wheaton, IL: Tyndale House, 1980), 83.
2. *Webster's New World Dictionary*, 3rd College Edition, (Simon & Schuster, 1991), s.v. "honor."
3. Ibid., s.v. "cherish."
4. Henry Cloud and John Townsend, *Boundaries in Marriage* (Grand Rapids, MI: Zondervan, 1999), 110.
5. Douglas E. Rosenau, *A Celebration of Sex* (Nashville: Nelson, 1994), 1.
6. Author unknown.
7. Clifford and Joyce Penner, "Intimate Service," *Focus on the Family Magazine*, (Colorado Springs, Focus on the Family, April 2004), 15.
8. Frederick Buechner as quoted in Cloud and Townsend, *Boundaries in Marriage*, 87.

The Word at Work Around the World

A vital part of Cook Communications Ministries is our international outreach, Cook Communications Ministries International (CCMI). Your purchase of this book, and of other books and Christian-growth products from Cook, enables CCMI to provide Bibles and Christian literature to people in more than 150 languages in 65 countries.

Cook Communications Ministries is a not-for-profit, self-supporting organization. Revenues from sales of our books, Bible curricula, and other church and home products not only fund our U.S. ministry, but also fund our CCMI ministry around the world. One hundred percent of donations to CCMI go to our international literature programs.

CCMI reaches out internationally in three ways:

· Our premier International Christian Publishing Institute (ICPI) trains leaders from nationally led publishing houses around the world.

· We provide literature for pastors, evangelists, and Christian workers in their national language.

· We reach people at risk—refugees, AIDS victims, street children, and famine victims—with God's Word.

Word Power, God's Power

Faith Kidz, RiverOak, Honor, Life Journey, Victor, NexGen — every time you purchase a book produced by Cook Communications Ministries, you not only meet a vital personal need in your life or in the life of someone you love, but you're also a part of ministering to José in Colombia, Humberto in Chile, Gousa in India, or Lidiane in Brazil. You help make it possible for a pastor in China, a child in Peru, or a mother in West Africa to enjoy a life-changing book. And because you helped, children and adults around the world are learning God's Word and walking in his ways.

Thank you for your partnership in helping to disciple the world. May God bless you with the power of his Word in your life.

For more information about our international ministries, visit www.ccmi.org.

Additional copies of *Sizzle!* and other Life Journey books
are available wherever good books are sold.

If you have enjoyed this book,
or if it has had an impact on your life,
we would like to hear from you.

Please contact us at:

LIFE JOURNEY BOOKS
Cook Communications Ministries, Dept. 201
4050 Lee Vance View
Colorado Springs, CO 80918

Or visit our Web site: www.cookministries.com

LIFE JOURNEY
Bringing Home the Message for Life